HORSEMANSHIP

AS IT IS TO-DAY

By

Sarah Bowes-Lyon

HORSEMANSHIP

35 drawings and colour plates

Horsemanship! Jumping! Showing!
Hunting! etc.

In two parts, for
PART I " begginers
" II " more expenenced

"Horsemanship as it is today" is a remarkable production for a lady of tender years. In one of her earlier remarks, in relation to the fitness for heaven of man and horse, one can perceive the driving force of her effort, viz. the true love of the Horse. One can but admire the accuracy with which she deals with the various details of Horsemanship, and also with the care of the horse. Although she cannot compete with a Herring or a Munnings, we see some graphic pictures in the art of riding, and in the picture of "the Horse and his points," it is very pleasing to see that she shows the shoulder neither straight nor loaded. The young writer covers a large field in connection with the horse and his management, as well as the correct form of equitation, and finally, I think her hints and advice should be of valuable help to the young aspirants who wish to excel in Horsemanship.

Strathmore & Kinghorne

Redbourn House
Redbourn
Herts

May 20th

Dear Mr Dent,

I am writing to thank you for so kindly saying that you will publish my book. I am so glad that you liked reading it and hope that you are as interested in horses as I am. I am sorry to think that I am now at school and have so very little time for writing, but I hope to do some more in the holidays. I like being at school very much though it is a pity that I am not able to ride my pony or go to any horse shows in the term.

With love and many thanks
from
Sarah

PREFACE.

DEAR READERS:

Before you read this little book I would like you to think, that, as well as for your own, it is also for your pony's, sake. When we look back, to those days when we first rode, we realise how very patient and gentle those ponies we were taught on were. We thought different then, and now, as I expect some of you experienced ones do, repent those times, when scoldings from our tongues would fall on those innocent twitching ears belonging those now beloved animals to whom we owe all our gratitued for horsemanship. Well one remembers, the clear gaze of the brown eyes, the pricked ears on the head,——held high, and the impatient twitch of the tail, of those noble steeds that bore us so gallantly at our first meet. It is those true hearted animals that teach us our first lessons,—— no master of horsemanship can ever teach as some of our early mounts taught us. Think of some of those miserable, unkept, cart horses, in the streets. The thin, meagre, rain sodden coat, through which protrode the bones, but, the soft white muzzle, and the clear dreamy eyes are still the same as when in better, bygone days.

The faithful beast is still waiting patiently,
—— with the traffic roaring past him,——
for his master,—— He comes, the cruel, rough
voice is heard as the brutal, merciless lash
falls with stinging force,—— the frame of
the horse quivers all over, but now the soft
ears are laid back and a glint of scorn
creeps into the mild eyes. Through all
unkindness that animal is still patient,
and still that old spark of fire comes
back to those eyes—— still that weary
frame unheeds those brutal blows......
Therefore let us raise our glasses and
drink to the long life and prosperity
of............................ "The Horse"!

"ALL HORSES ARE FIT FOR
            HEAVEN,
    BUT FEW MEN."

S. Bowes-Lyon

CONTENTS.

ILLUSTRATIONS.

continued

✦ Pen and ink.

I DEDICATE THIS BOOK
To: My mother and father and
Miss Clay, _____ Jaffie, and Devon,
to whom I owe all my gratitued
for the know ledge of all that
is written in the following pages
of this book. And, also, of all the
readers who have been bored with
it to the one who never showed
resentment.

"A thing worth
doing.
Is worth doing
well"!

Sarah Bowes-Lyon.

Begun at the age of twelve at
Redbourn House

PART 1.
for begginers.
Seat, Kit, Hands, Paces Saddling, Mounting etc.

CHAPTER I
"Riding Kit"

RIDING KIT

Hat --- a soft felt hat is best, for usual riding and hacking purposes though for hunting and jumping it is safer to wear a bowler or some hard hat. with a piece of elastic at the back to hold it on by.

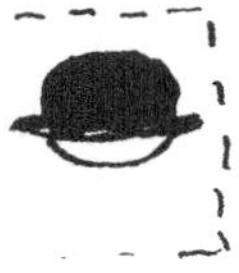

Stock --- One only needs a stock for hunting really and one can either have a tie or not ^thing^ at all as it is not a great necessity.

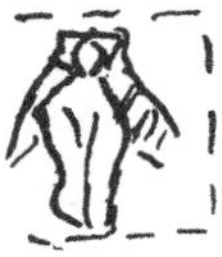

Coat --- For the winter, and hunting one of course wants a pretty thick coat to Keep out all the cold, and it should have a slit at the back.

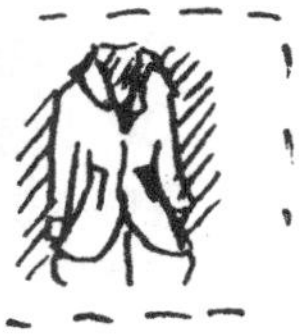

Breeches --- Breeches are best, made from measurements, and they should fit well round the hips and legs, with not too much sag in the back, and Jodhpors should fit closely all down the legs. (Note) (Both breeches and Jodhpors wear better if with a strip of leather inside the knee)

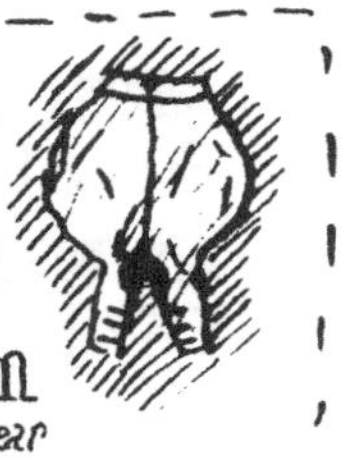

Leggings --- Leggins must be fitted well, or they are both untidy and uncomfortable. the plain brown leather Kind, or white padded ones are best, and though top boots are not so suitable they are quite useful for hunting.

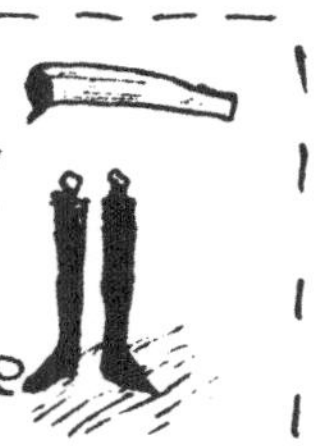

Gloves – – – – Cream coloured string gloves are the most usefull for all times, though the "Holdness Hunt" have the best kind for hunting, as they are made with warm stuff, and some other specialy for holding reins with.

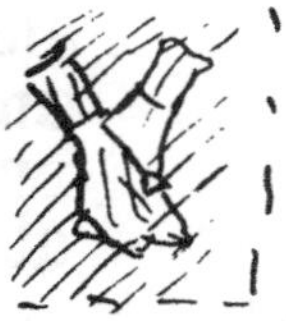

Crop – – – – – A crop is generaly only used for hunting and as one should not take off the "thong" to use it with only the keep, it is much better and more useful to have a stick or Malacca cane both for ridding and showing as it is not the right thing, to ride with anything but a stick, also, cutting whips are only used by jockeys.

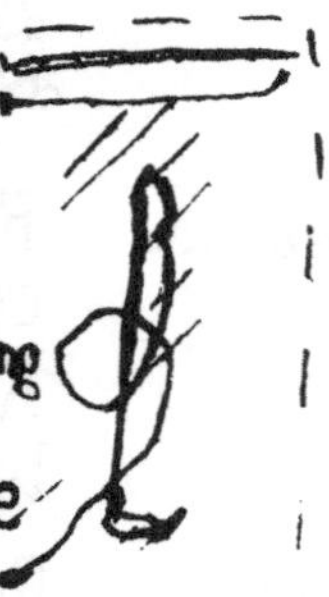

Spurs – – – – there are so many morals and stories about people using spurs that I think we will quote these well known lines –
"Spurs should be worn by no one except one man in a hundred and then he should never use them"! . .

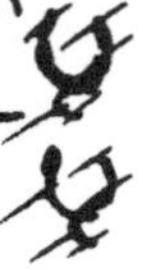

"THE HUNTING CROP.

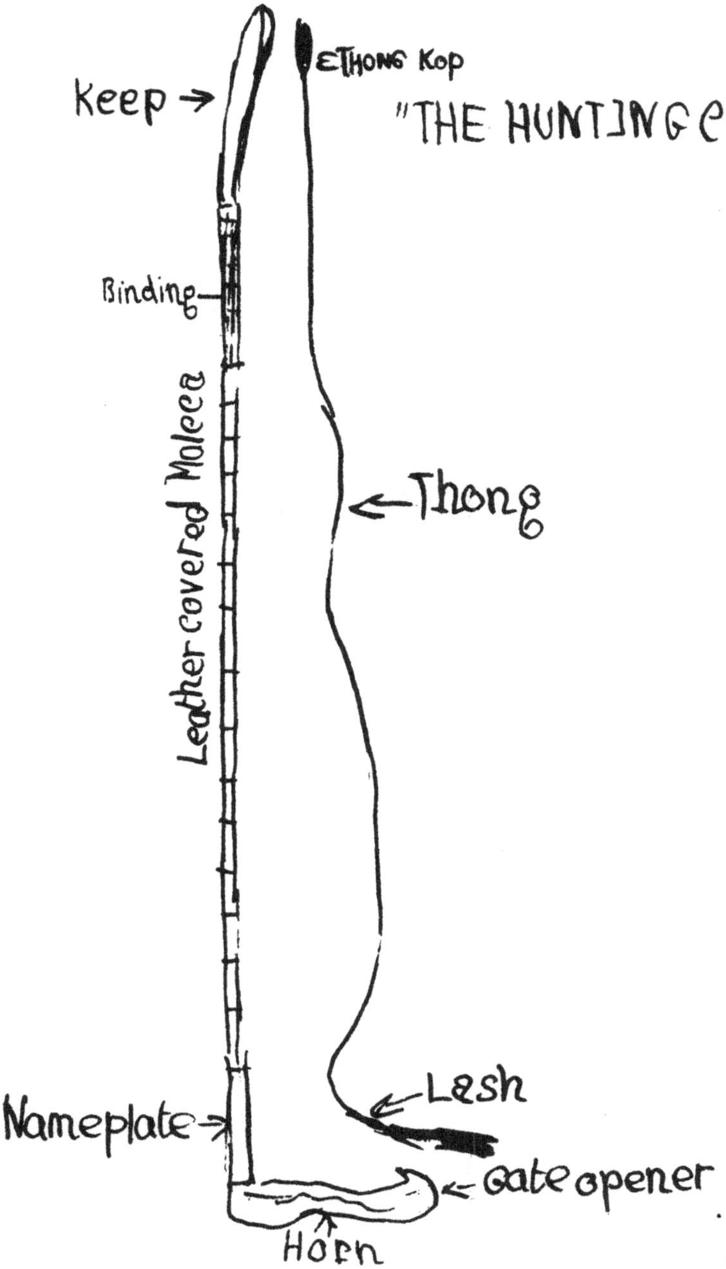
THONG KOP
Keep
Binding
Leather covered Malecca
Thong
Lash
Nameplate
Gate opener
Horn

CHAPTER II

"The points of a horse"

– – – – – – – – –

THE POINTS OF A HORSE.

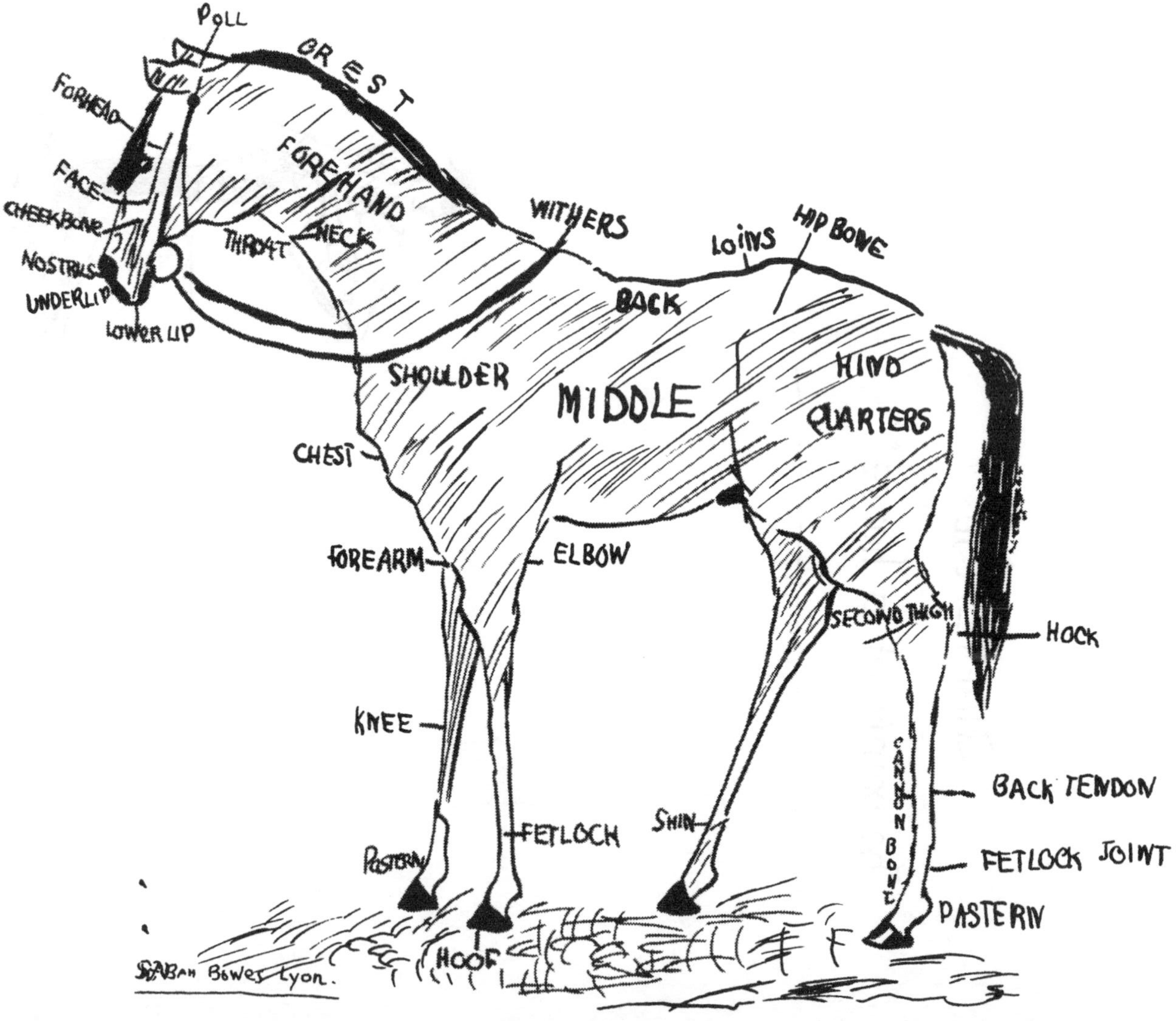
POLL
CREST
FORHEAD
FACE
CHEEKBONE
NOSTRILS
UNDERLIP
LOWER LIP
THROAT
NECK
FOREHAND
WITHERS
LOINS
HIP BONE
BACK
SHOULDER
MIDDLE
HIND
QUARTERS
CHEST
FOREARM
ELBOW
SECOND THIGH
HOCK
KNEE
CANNON BONE
BACK TENDON
FETLOCK
SHIN
FETLOCK JOINT
PASTERN
PASTERN
HOOF
SARAH Bowes Lyon.

THE POINTS OF YOUR PONY

This chapter is not only for people
who dont know the points of the horse
but also for people who do know, as
one can never stop learning all the
different names, in fact one learns
them at each stage, and so on, till
one time they come in very useful,
not counting it as being most
intresting, for instance, say, if your
father was going to give you a pony,
he would very likely say " first, you
must learn the names of a ponies
points, do you know them"? - - -
what would happen if you did'nt? __
well, here they are for you to try
and fix in your memory _____

the .. POLL ... is just between the two
ears if you place your hand there
you will feel a little hump,

FORHEAD .... a little bit above the eyes,
— just the same as our own!

FACE ... is just below the eyes.

CHEEK BONE —... is on the side of the
face it feels like a thin little ledge
if you run your hand down it.

NOSTRILS..... are a very delicate part of a pony as of course it is where he breathes through exactly the same as our noses' and we dont like anyone pinching them either, do we? well then, never do a thing to your pony that you' would'nt like youreself...

UNDERLIP.... is just below the nostrils, and the

LOWERLIP... just below that, then we have to look up a bit, to find the ____

THROAT.. that is very easy, I expect you to know that!

NECK... is a little below the "Throat." Now we have got to go right up to the top and begin again at the ____

CREST.. which goes all along the top of his mane. and below him, a word you should know, "which side is the? ____

FOREHAND..... "on your left when mounted," its very easy to forget! Now for the ____

WITHERS... you can see them just in front of the saddle when mounted, just like a jump.

the BACK..... is where we sit. the next
point is very important_____

LOINS... the most delicate part of a
horse or pony, so if a wet day at a
meet, etc, allways cover him up there

HIPBONE......is just below the "Loins"
there is hardly need to ask if you know
where the_____

HINDQUARTERS—— are? I will leave that
to you!

SECOND THIGH....is just above the_____

HOCK...you have all <u>heard</u> of that word?
the ——

BACK TENDON...is just behind and the

CANNON BONE....just in front.

CHEST... below the——

SHOULDER,.. the —

FORARM......in front of the ——

ELBOW.... the——

KNEE .... above the——

PASTERN,..the pastern above the HOOF, and the shin
is by itself....you'll have to learn these off by heart!
the picture will help you and dont forget them as
soon as you have them learnt.........!

←—·—·—··—·—·—·—→

CHAPTER III
" Bridling, Saddling, Mounting etc.

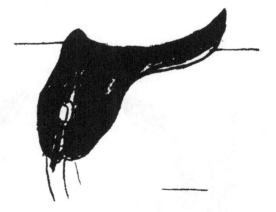

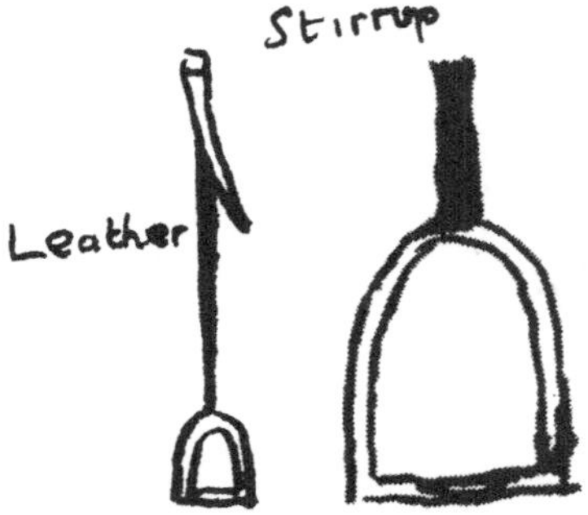
Stirrup
Leather

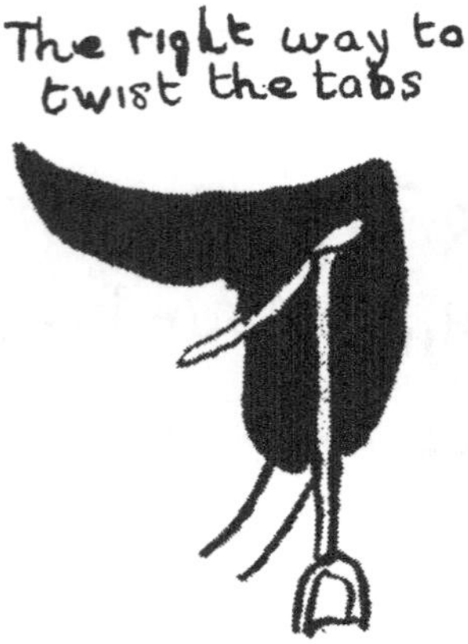
The right way to
twist the tabs

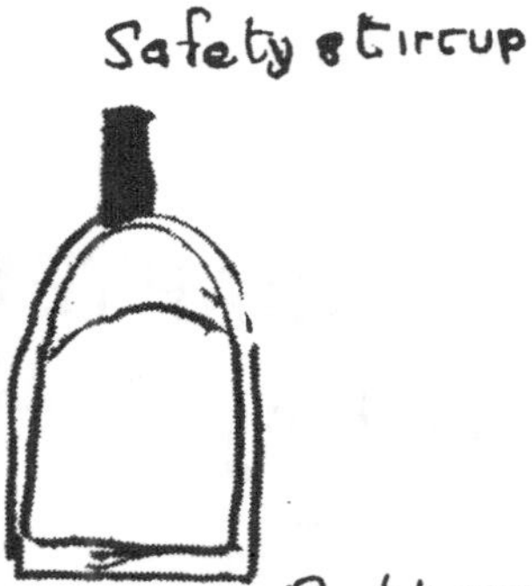
Safety stirrup

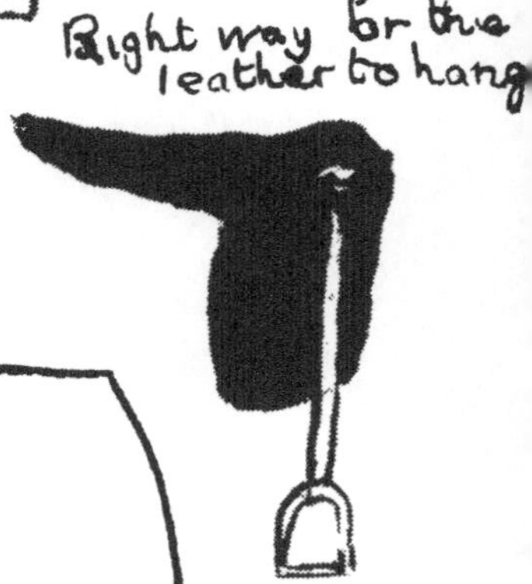
Right way for the
leather to hang

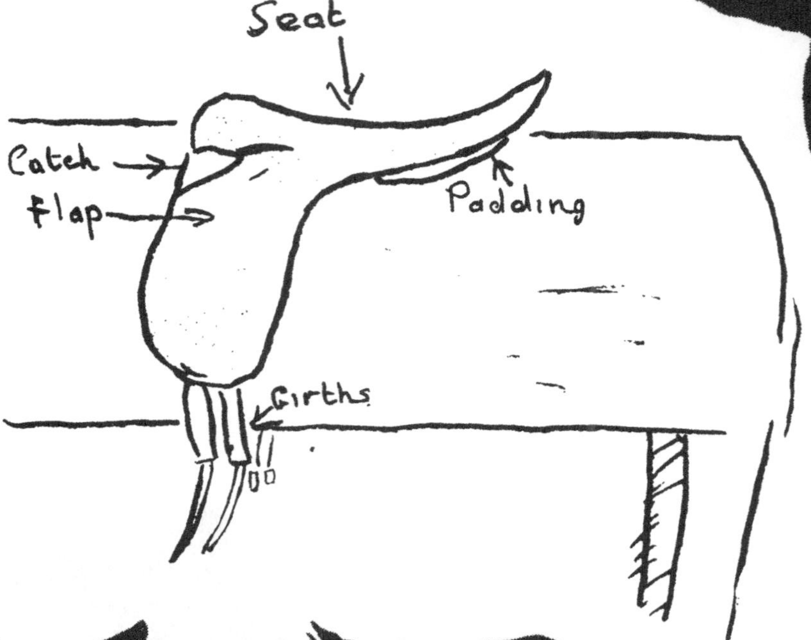
Seat
Catch
Flap
Padding
Girths

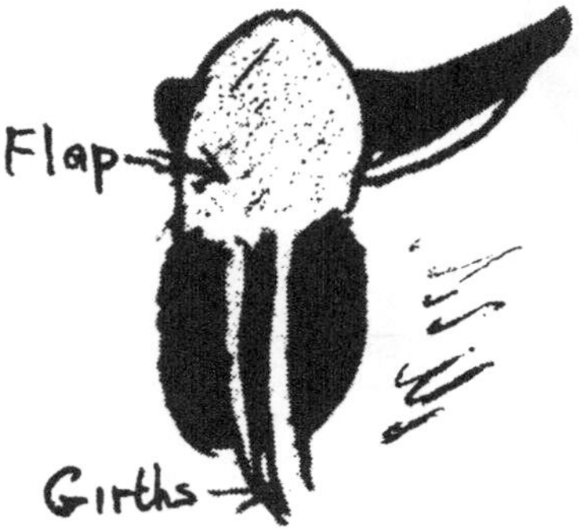
Flap
Girths

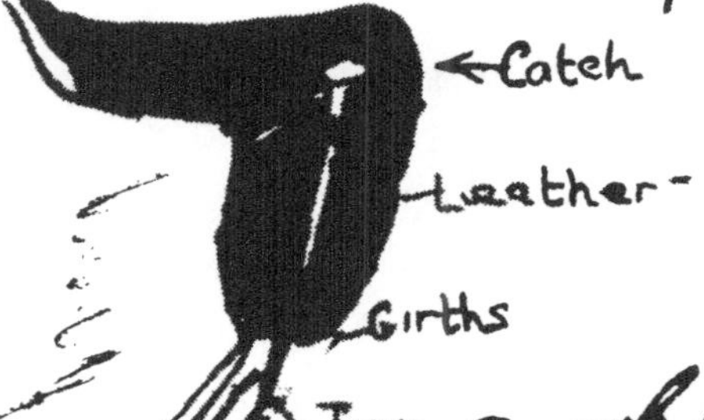
Catch
Leather
Girths
Iron

If you are one of those lucky beginners
who have your own pony you must know
how to do the following:

To "SADDLE" him, stand on the nearside, if
he is a bit figety it is better to tie him
up or get some one to hold his head.
Pick the saddle up and place it gently on his
back then shift it politely into the right possihon
which should be, not too far forward and not
too far back. Now hold the saddle of the near
girth with your left hand to steady it, then,
with the right hand stretch under, and catch
hold of, the other girth, draw it up to your side
and slip it through the buckle, tightening
them till you can just slip two fingers through.
But, mind you tighten your girths before
mounting! The next thing to do is to —
"BRIDLE" your pony, but you must be very very
gentle or he will tell you what you did the
next time!... take the bridle and undo the
nose, and cheek bands. When you are ready,
slip off the halter, place your right arm round
his neck to rest on his nose, with your left
arm held near the cheek of the bit insert
your thum just where his lips end, he
will open his mouth and you can slip the
bit in, while the right hand holds the head

piece by the cheek bits , when you have inserted the bit, put the reins and head band behind his ears, do up the nose band and cheek straps. You aught to be able to push your fist through the cheek strap. "STIRRUPS". slide the clip along the bar and adjust to right length. When you know how to do all these things we will go on to —

"MOUNTING"... Pick up the reins with your left hand and face his tale taking hold of the stirrup leather low down with your right. Place your left foot well in the stirrup and take hold of the saddle near the back. —— give a spring from the right toe pressing well upon the stirrup. —— lift your bent leg carefuly over the back of the saddle. —— and drop gently beside the other leather, and insert foot in the iron. to—

"DISMOUNT" take both feet out of stirrups still holding reins, swing the right leg over back of saddle and slide to the ground.

Now, perhaps if you can only just reach to get on your pony you will not want to get off again if you have forgotten to tighten your girths, so it is very useful to know how to alter them "mounted" as seen on page 20.

Hold your reins and stick with your "right" hand, and put your left leg as far <u>forward</u> as possible, with your left hand pull up the "flap," and rest against arm, then catch hold of one of the girth tabs and pull up to the hole wanted. Then you must know how to alter your "stirrups" mounted. put your leg as far <u>back</u> as you can, holding your reins, with the hand the other side of the stirrup you are altering, as "opposite page. Take hold of the "tab" with the other hand and alter to right hole, keeping your foot <u>in</u> the stirrup all the time even when altering your girths.

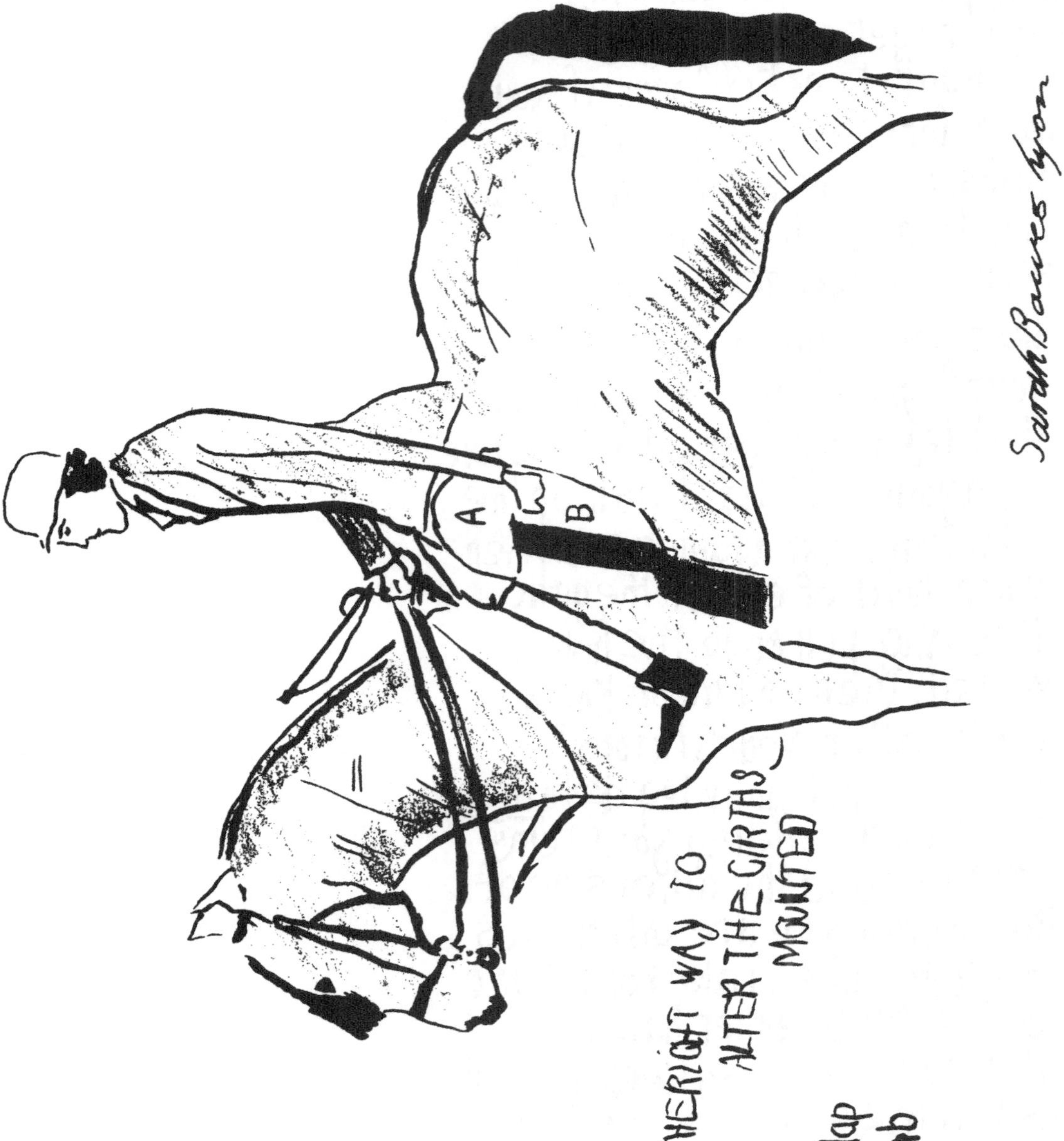
A
B
Sarah Bowes Lyon

THE RIGHT WAY TO ALTER THE GIRTHS MOUNTED

A Flap
B Tab

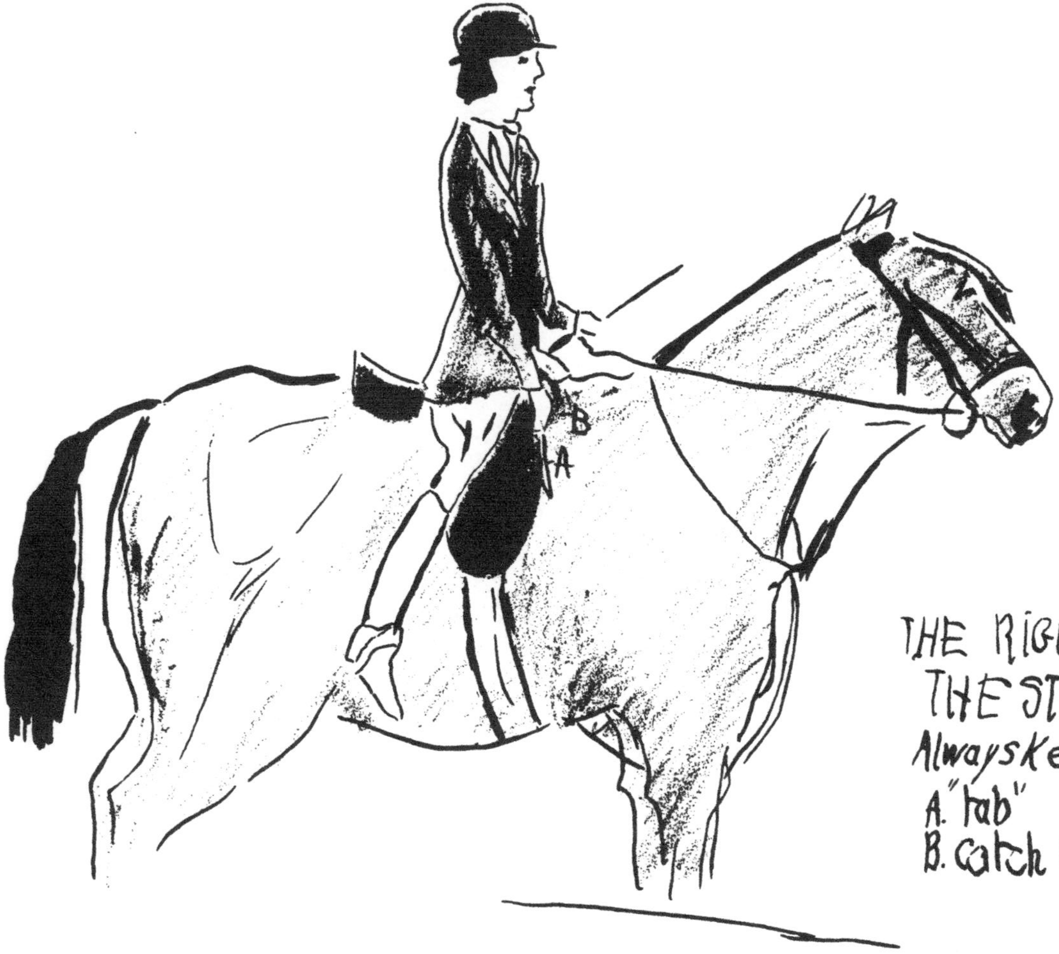
B
A

THE RIGHT WAY TO ALTER THE STIRRUPS MOUNTED.

Always keep foot in iron

A. "tab"

B. catch flap"

CHAPTER IV

"HANDS"

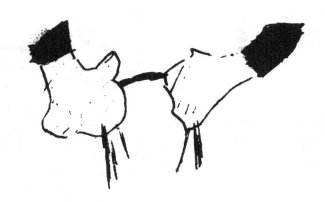

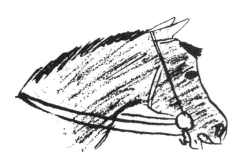

BAD HANDS.
This pony had a rider with <u>bad</u> hands. you can see his is not happy by his expression and open mouth.

<u>GOOD HANDS.</u>
Note. This pony's mouth is closed. He is comfortable. He is going up to his bridle but is not fighting against it.

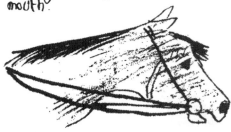

THE UNBALANCED PONY
Low head and unhappy expression of the <u>unbalanced</u> pony he has to lean on the bit for safty

THE BALANCED PONY
Head held high with a proud look. but although <u>balanced</u> he is still not so comfortable as the pony with a <u>good</u> rider.

HANDS

You have often heard about people with good hands, so you won't want them to say you have bad ones. Good hands are naturaly gifted, but there is no need to say that one shouldn't have light hands, which with time and practice can grow into good hands. What I mean by light hands is, that you are not always "pulling" and "nagging" at your pony's mouth, but can manage him with out always "holding on". Lots of people have gone out riding on perfectly quiet horses and the same old story is told again " That horse of yours pulls like the dickens, I simply can't hold him" perhaps if you said to those persons "Have you tried not always "pulling" at his mouth"?

A GOOD SEAT ASTRIDE

the answer is "No", well, then, if you
tell them to drop their reins and
not always "nag", they will have
no more trouble! To have good
hands is one of the greatest
things in horsemanship, and one
to be proud of, the "horse and
rider are as one". On the next
page you will see how to hold
your reins, you must imagine
them something very delicate
that would break at once if
you jerked them, and the same
with your pony's mouth, the lighter
the touch the more quickly and
willing he will obey, and until all
riders get this firmly into their minds
they will have great difficulty in
managing their horses, and never
have good hands. Yet on the other
hand you must not have your
reins so slack that your pony

28 Fig1. Right way to hold the reins

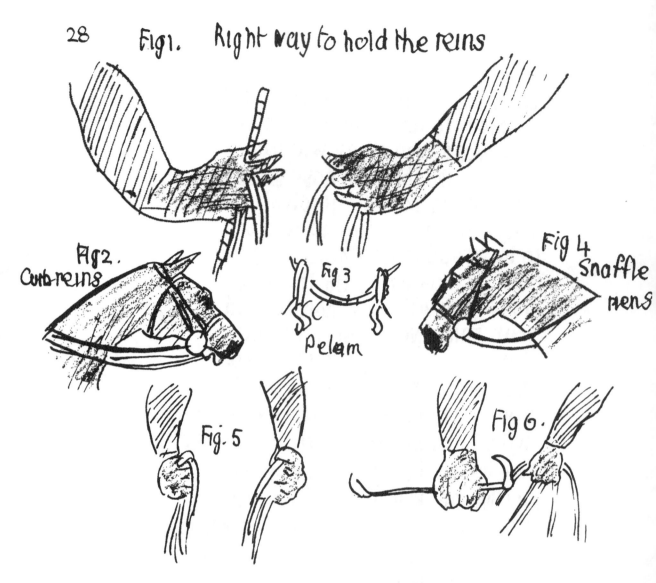

Fig 2.
Curb reins

Fig 3
Pelam

Fig 4
Snaffle
reins

Fig. 5

Fig 6.

Fig 5. Wrong way to
hold curb reins

Fig 6. Wrong way to
hold reins and crop

Sarah Reeves Ryor.

goes just where he wants.
You must just be able to feel
that his mouth is there, and
a firm but gentle touch.
If you look on page 24 you
will see what a horse looks like
with a good and bad rider. To
"balance" your pony, say, at the
trot, take a firm touch on the
reins, (don't ever let him go along
with slack reins so that his head
is drooped down as in the 3rd fig.
page 15, as he is "unbalanced,"
one often sees cart horses like
this, and it is dangerous as well,
he might easily slip.) Then aply
the legs till an even steady pace
is reached, still holding his head
well up. If your pony is well "balanced"
he will be much more likely to win
at shows than one who is not.

The way you hold your hands, too,
is always noted and it helps
greatly with your seat, espesialy
        begginers, as, when they canter
if they keep their hands low, their
bodies do not rise so. When you
have taken hold of the reins,
bend your wrists inwards so that
your thums are strait
acrose your body, and let them
just touch. Then drop hands down.
till just not touching the front
of the saddle, and draw back
still the lips of your thumbs are
just touching your body. This
is the correct possition for the
walk, for the trot, shorten reins
till hands are just above the
front of the saddle. For the
canter, draw back hands just
about an inch from front of
saddle. For the gallop. shorten reins
till hands rest just in front of
the saddle, or, where his mane
ends.

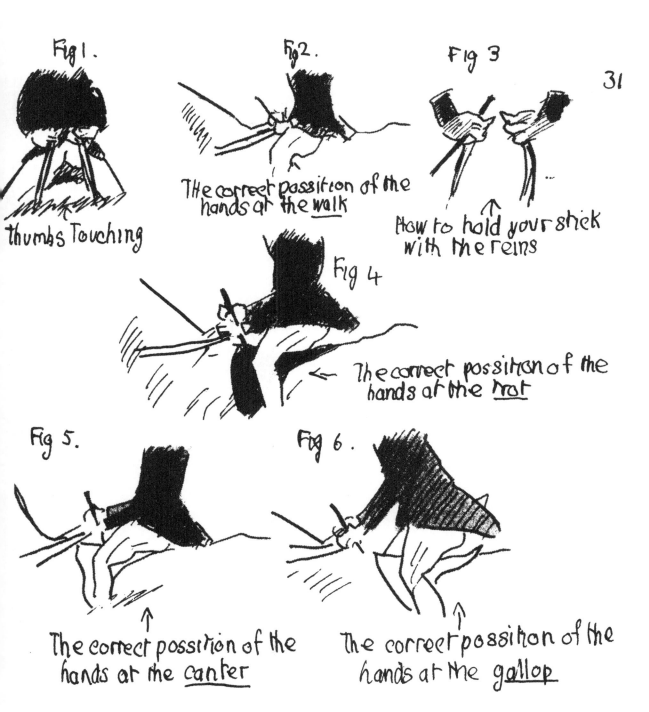

Fig 1.

thumbs Touching

Fig 2.

The correct possition of the hands at the walk

Fig 3

How to hold your stick with the reins

Fig 4

The correct possition of the hands at the trot

Fig 5.

The correct possition of the hands at the canter

Fig 6.

The correct possition of the hands at the gallop

Sarah Llowellyn

The Seat
V

"a copy for all riders as a 'good' seat."

The Seat

When you have bridled and saddled
your pony you mount as shown in
Chapter III, now let your legs hang
naturaly, and you will get the possition
as in Fig 1. on the next page, then if
you draw your leg, back, and lean
slightly more forward you will get
the "Natural" seat "modified" seen in
Fig 2. and that is the possition we
get all the different seats from. Now,
when you have tried all these
possitions without stirrups you
will now have to know how to
get the right length for them.
"Stirrups" A good way is to ride a bit till
you get well down in the saddle
and then feel the irons knocking
against your ankles, another is,
to, keep your feet in the stirrups
and when you stand up, your

Natural seat.

Fig 1.

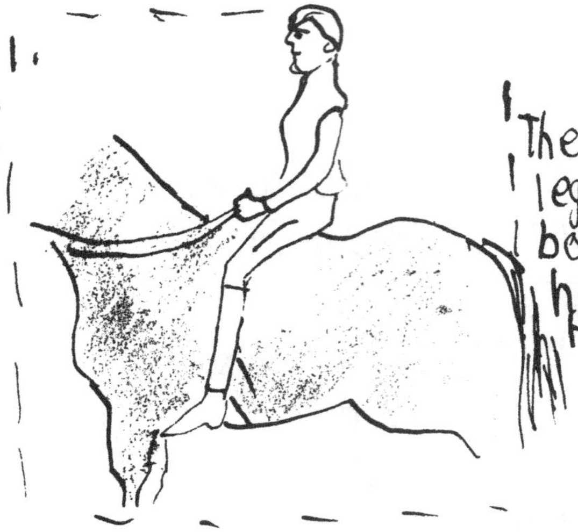

The "Natural" seat, the legs are forward, and the body throw back so that he can balance. Note the girth line.

The "Natural" seat modified. The legs are drawn back which results in the knee being raised and the body in a more forward possition than Fig 1. Note. the difference in space between the girths

Fig 2.

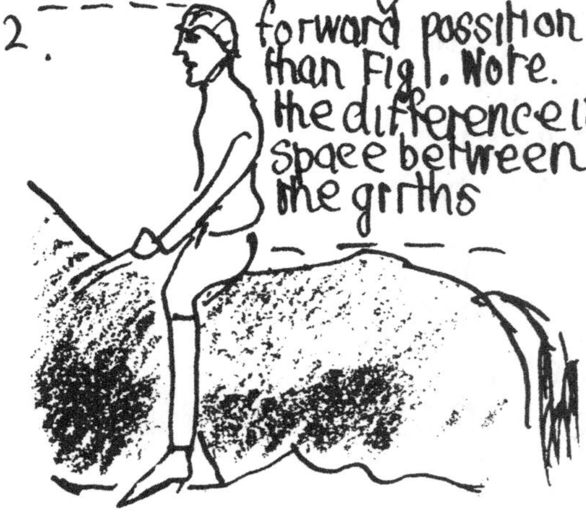

The "Modified" seat with saddle and stirrups, which bends the knee still further. Note the raised toe and leg covering girth. (compare with Fig 2.

Fig 3.

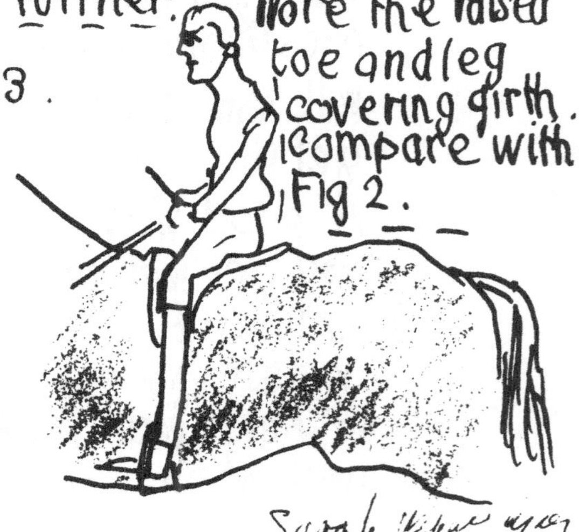

Sarah [illegible]

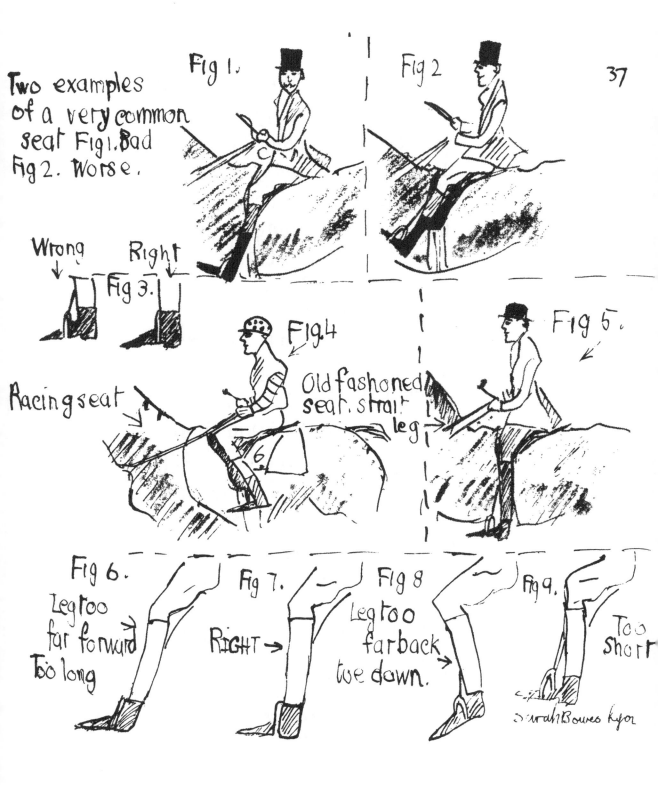

Two examples of a very common seat Fig 1. Bad Fig 2. Worse.

Fig 1.

Fig 2

Wrong   Right
Fig 3.

Racing seat

Fig 4

Old fashioned seat. strait leg

Fig 5.

Fig 6.
Leg too far forward Too long

Fig 7.
RIGHT →

Fig 8
Leg too far back toe down.

Fig 9.
Too short

Sarah Bowes Lyon

fork, just clears the bow of the saddle, But, it is better to ride with stirrups too long than too short. If you want a good seat you must sit up as strait as you can with your legs hanging strait down from the knees it is a very good way to get the legs in the right possition, if you can just see the tips of your toes over your knees but you must sit up strait. Always keep your hands as low as possible and your heels well down. Lots of people take up their own seats (some of which are given on the next page) and look very ludicous so I think the "Hunting" seat is much the best for both children and grown ups. The plainer the better. It is very useful to learn these lines:

"Your head and your heart
keep up!
Your hands and your heels keep
down!
Your knees dig into your horse's sides!
And your elbows into your own!"
Jocky Chiffney

Different seats.

On the next page the "Hunting"
and "Racing" seat can be seen.
The difference between these
is, that, the jockey has his knees
level with the line of the saddle,
while the other rides much longer.
The "Hunting" seat is for "practical"
work and is the most useful of
all seats. The "old fashioned" seat
seen on the opisite page is seldom
used now, as one does not often
see, a rider riding so long, or,
with the stirrup on the ball of the
foot nowadays we ride with it
"right up". And, his knee is almost
strait, which, although good for
the balance, is not nearly so
comfortable. This fashion is
sometimes tried on beginners
to make them sit up, and balance
themselves better, while the stirrup
on the toe keeps the heels down.

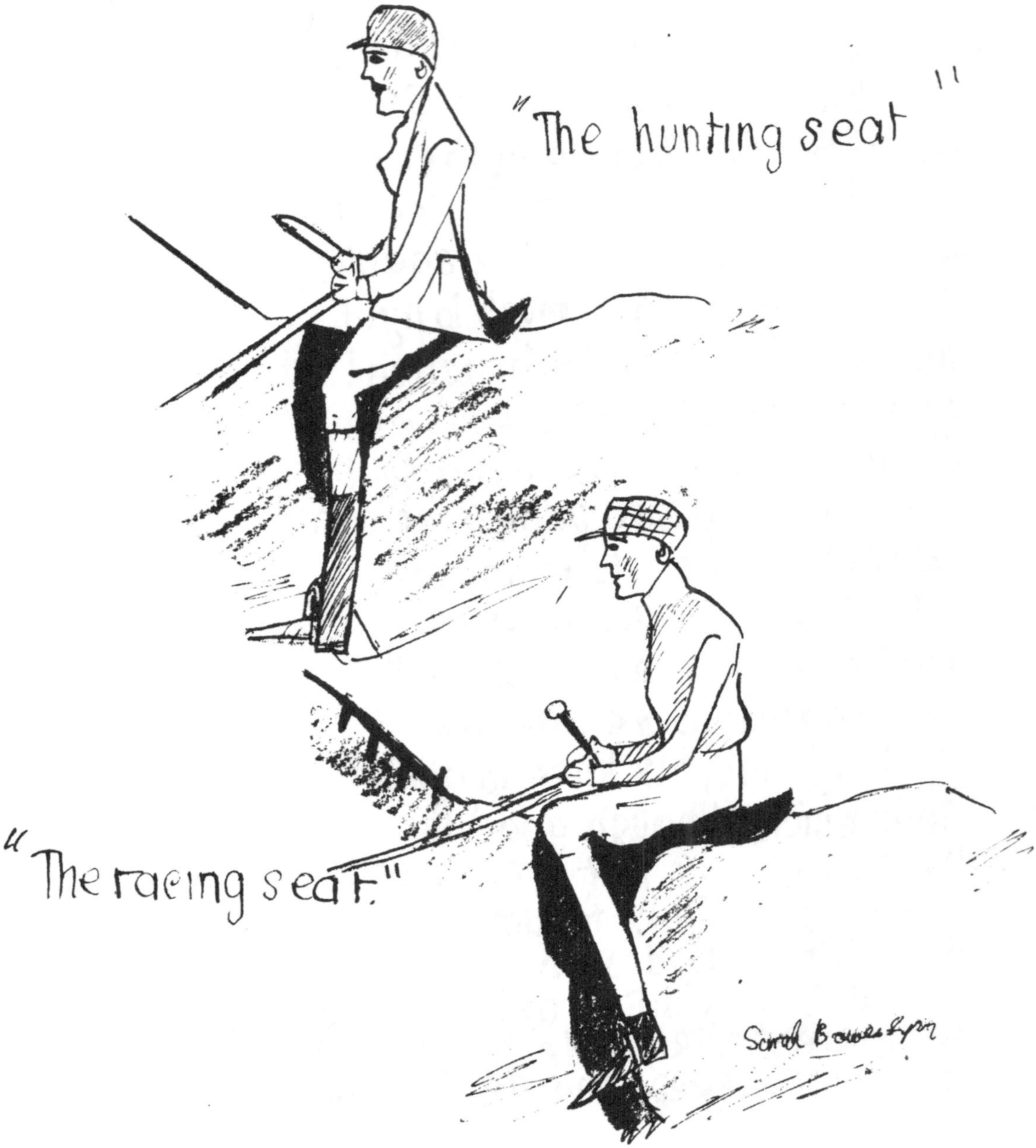
"The hunting seat"
"The racing seat."

CHAPTER VI

"Paces"

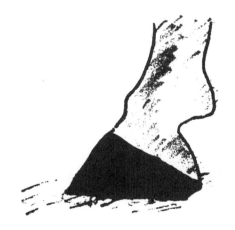

"Walk" the slowest pace of the horse,

"Trotting" there are two kinds, the "jog" and "proper". The "jog" trot is between a quick walk and a trot, and is a very common habbit and rather uncomfortable for those who are not aquanted with it. To trot "properly", shorten reins and apply the legs till a steady pace is reached.

To "Canter". Get a firm touch on the reins, apply legs and lean slightly back.

To "Gallop" Shorten reins, ease your pony's head till he stretches out, lean rather forward and keep him going steadyly. If a fast gallop, catch hold of his head, lean forward, and ease up in the stirrups. To stop, draw back the hands, press well on the stirrups and lean slightly back, if he does not give in, give a good pull, then ease the reins, go on doing this till he stops.

"THE BRIDLE"

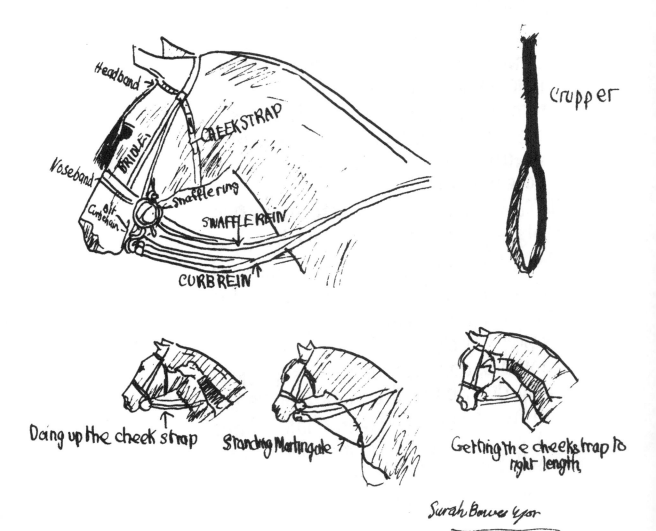

Headband

CHEEKSTRAP

BRIDLE,

Noseband

Bit
Curbchain

Snaffle ring

SNAFFLE REIN

CURB REIN

Crupper

Doing up the cheek strap

Standing Martingale

Getting the cheekstrap to right length

Sarah Bower Lyon

But, if your pony is hard to
stop, he very likely has a bad
and hard mouth, and will grow
into a "puller" which a child or
begginer should never have, it
will wreck their confidence.
When ever your pony gives in
to the pressure of the reins,
always drop your hands and ease
his mouth, the world known rule
of "horsemanship",
"BENDING". Ride round in circles.
To turn to the right rest the left
rein against your pony's neck and
use your left heel, leaning towards
the right.
To turn to the left, rest the right
rein on your pony's neck, and use
the right heel, leaning towards
the left. It is also very good
practice to do figure eights etc.
Cantering, trotting, and so on.

Up the hill hurry me
Down the hill hurry me not
On the flat let me go!

PART II

For the more experienced, or, those beginers who have already been through PART I

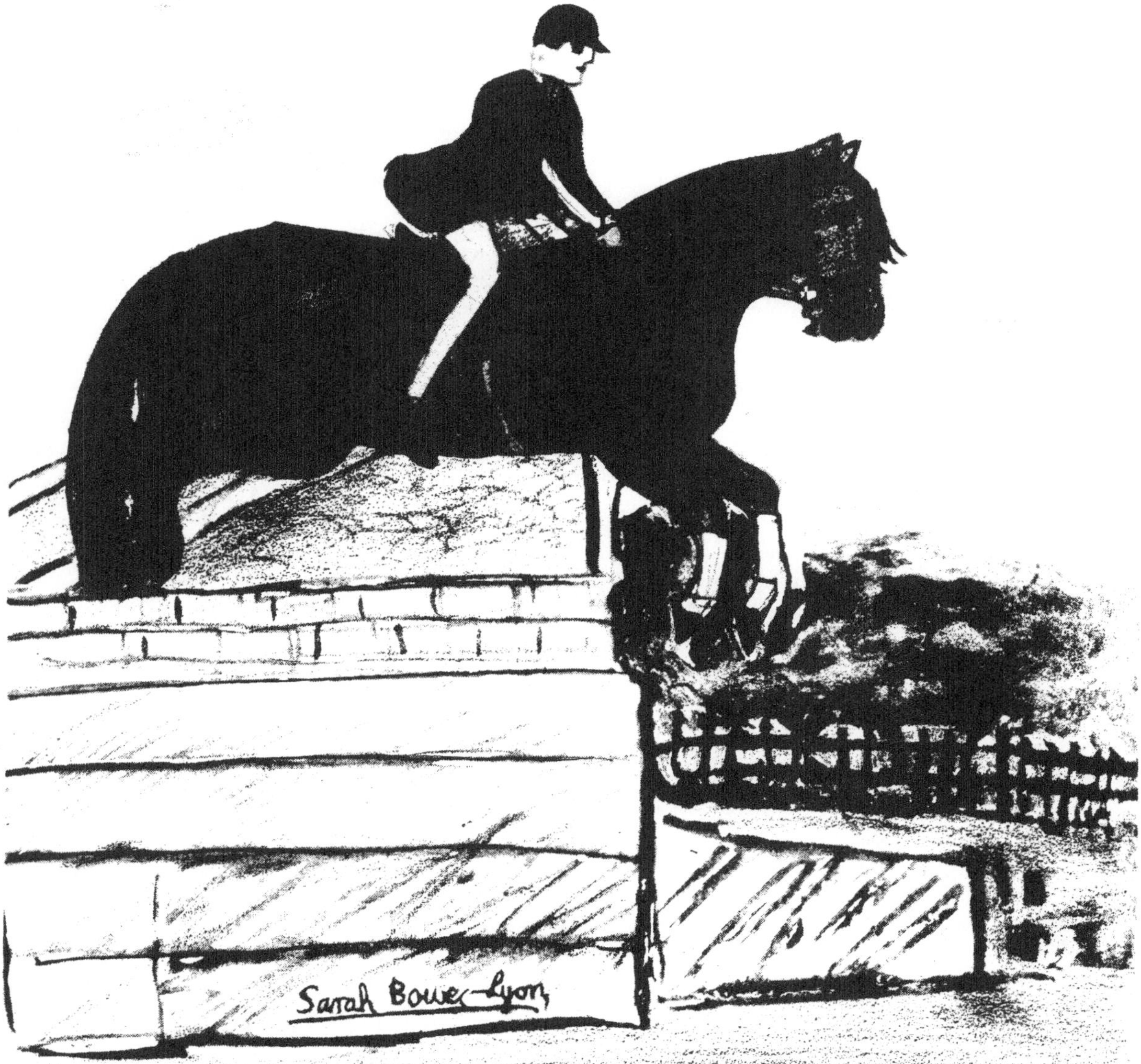
Sarah Bowes-Lyon

CHAPTER VII

"Jumping"

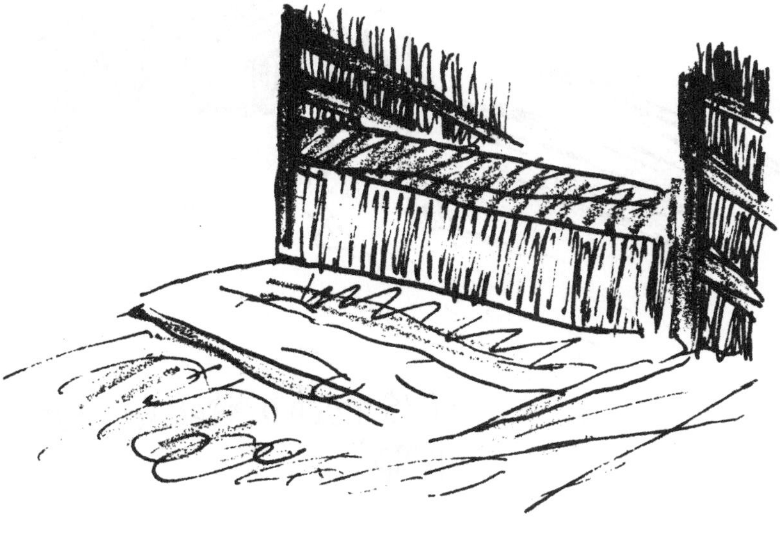

50

'The leap, the rise, from the springy
turf!'
The light shock landing! ————
Adam Lindsay Gordon

"It is much better to start with a tiny jump."

Jumping!, the word alone gives a
thrill to any child that has ever
tasted that grand feeling! even
one who has had many years
of experience cannot help having
a flicker of pride in his eye as
he recalls, those days when he came
down bump, on a shetland pony's
back, and saying to himself, "that's
my first jump"! and back again, to
the row of cups on the mantlepiece,
which, with their gleaming faces,
tell of bygone jumping feats! ah!
woebegone reader, who has never
tried to jump! who has never felt that thrill!
as his horse clears! the light shock
landing! and the fall!—for, no one is
ashamed when they find themself
in the mud, instead of the saddle,
even world known proffesionals
rememper back in their lives
of at least one hearty good fall,
and sometimes I may say,—with pride!

Post and rails are very good for practicing over.

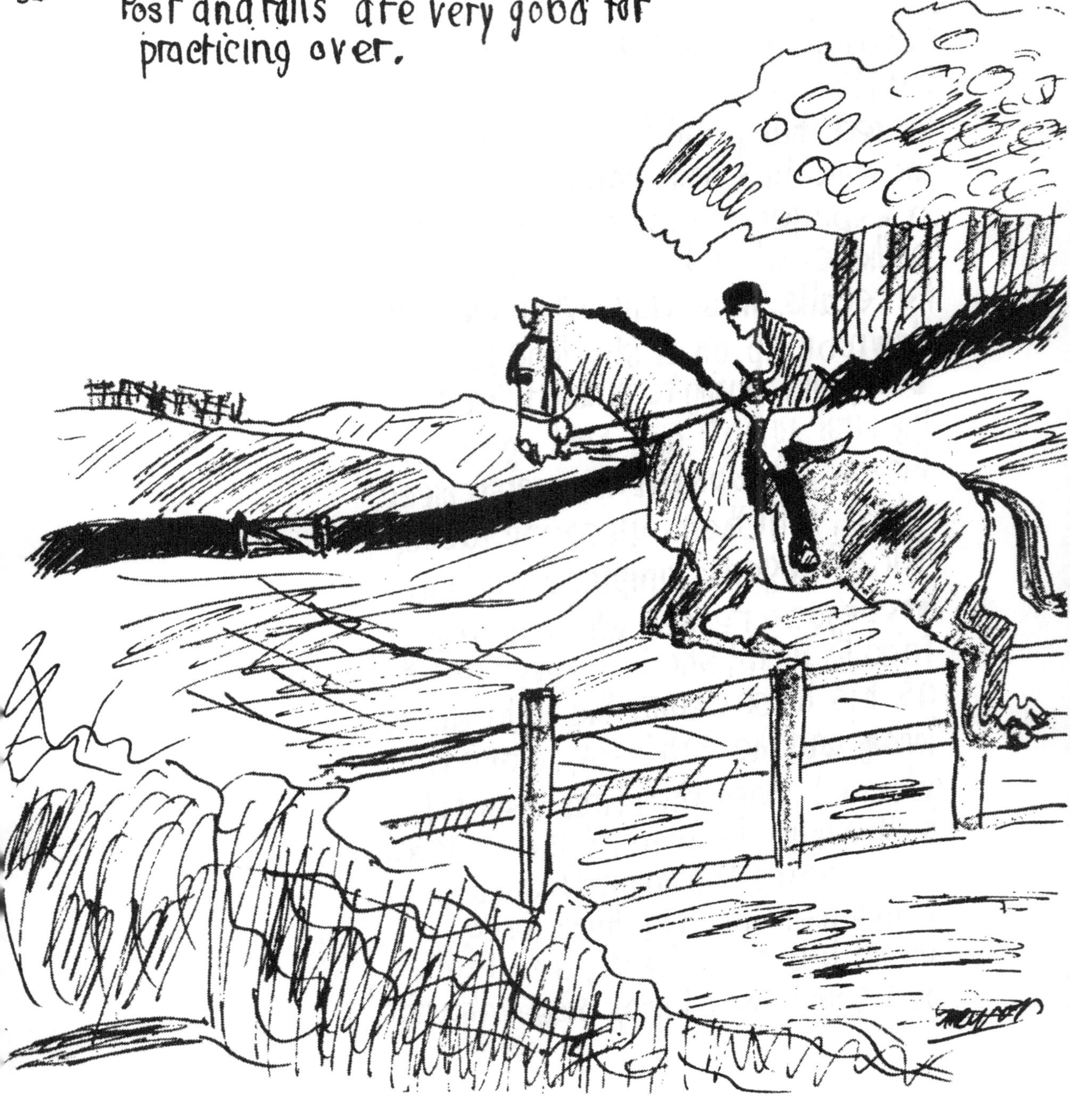

Now then you boys and girls hurry
up and try your first jump! you
need not be afraid as on no account
must you go over a jump more
than two feet, "start low, and work
gradualy up," slow but sure. You'll
then be able to say what you think
about jumping! At first you will
want to lean rather too far forward,
but, gradualy, the right possition
will come by practice. You do not
want to "hang "on" to your pony's
mouth, but just a firm anough
hold to keep him steady, trot
up to about a few feet from the
jump first, then let him go!,
keep his head strait, so that he
does not "run out," then hold tight!,
and before you can say "christopher
Columbus"! you will find yourself
the other side, and, if all is well,
——— in the saddle!

Horses seldom like stone walls.

"THE JUMPS" should be placed in a fairly large dry
paddoek or field, and, should consist of, at

first, for begginers, of rails and brush fences,
the latter should have a strip of board about
a foot from the top on the side you are
going to jump, so that the horse can't just
"brush" through them, and the rails should
be made of hollow wood, as, if they are
solid, your pony will crack his hoofs if
he hits it, also they should be fixed to
fly off at the least touch, so you won't
come a cropper! It is great fun to
have an "imatation" steeplechase corse running
through two or three fields, and the
jumps made, according to the hight you
can jump, some could be, for instance,
a low gap in the "hedge" "filled up,"
some bars put across an empty
gateway, or, if you have a boundry
fence of posts and rails to take the
top rail of one of the lengths out.
And as well as being the greatest
fun, you will find it very good practice!.

56

Fig 1.   Brush. made of Gorse.   Rails   Fig 2.

Gap. trimmed.   Fig 4.   Old Gateway
Fig 3.

Post and rails cut down.   CUT AND LAYED.
Fig 5   Fig 6.

BRUSH   Stone wall.

Fig 7.   Fig 8.

" Making your own Jumps" is realy most exciteing! — except when they fall down! and you're underneath! But you must make them strong anough not to! and if you have plenty of wood and stuff to make them with, it is a great occupation, specialy for the holidays. Well, lets say we will start at the "Brush" fig 1. First of all, you must get plenty of the above, the picture shows you quite a good hight, but you can always cut it of course to your size. Get two good solid posts, and bang in at about 6ft apart, but they must be on an even line or your jump will come crooked! Now stick each branch about an inch into the ground, do a single row first, and then get thicker. After you have done this, hammer a nail into one side, of the posts, get the bit of board, and balance it on these. If you want 'wings' of the same, stick some high bamboo canes into the ground, and twine the branches in and out of them.

Fig 1. is of gorse, and made in exactly the same way as fig. 7. only rather wider. In fig. 2. is rails, resting on the nails in the posts. Fig 3. is a rough hedge trimmed. Fig. 4. is put up in the same way as Fig 2. Fig. 5. is the top bar of a "post and rails" taken away. Fig 6. is what we call "cut and layed". Fig. 7. has already been shown how to make, and Fig. 8. is like the stone walls in Northumberland. Now, we must give a few lines to the kinds of hedges in different counties. In Warwickshire you will find out hunting the hedges are very easy for "scimming" over as they consist of either clipped "brush" or "cut and layed", which are not much more than 3 ft. At Melton too, they are all "clipped". The Hertfordshire hedges are thick and wide, with many a "blind ditch". and the "Percy Hunt" in Northumberland, have chiefly stone walls.

CHAPTER VIII
"Showing"· · · ·

"Rosettes"

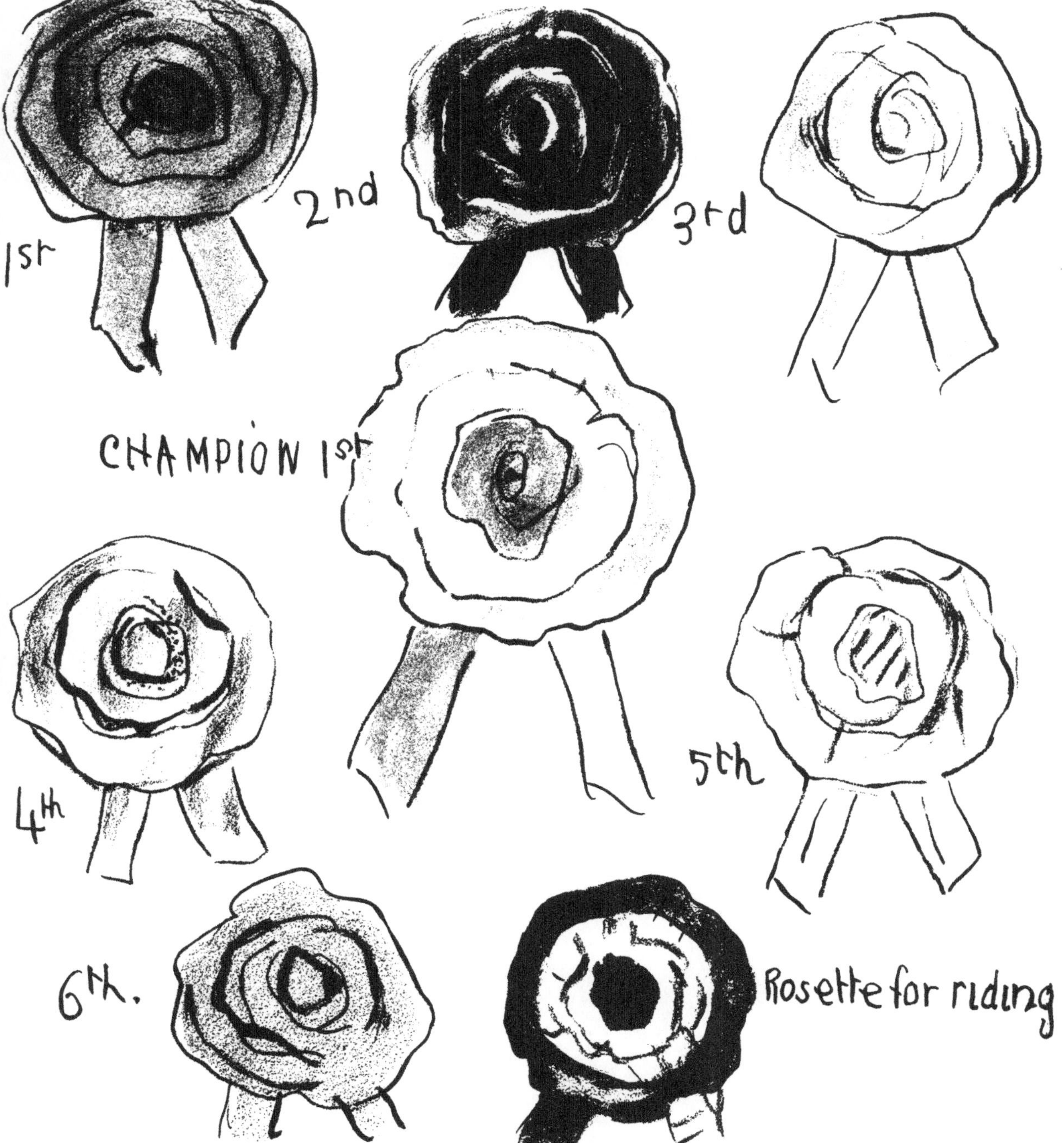
1st
2nd
3rd
CHAMPION 1st
4th
5th
6th.
Rosette for riding

SHOWING

Showing is an art by itself, and needs both skillfulness, and knowledge, to be able to do it well. It is a very good thing, if **you** are not riding, to watch carefuly those who are experienced, in the ring, and you will see how they take everything with coolness as it comes, you must never get excited or your pony will too, it is hopeless. And also, watch their manners in the ring too, for this counts above everything, and the Judges notice it. Never push, be content to be where you are, help other people out of difficulty when you can, and, above all, do not gaze about you, pay attention only, to your pony and yourself. When you first enter the ring, wait till those who want to get in front, are past, you then take your place, the Judge will take just as much

"CHAMPION CUP"
FOR THE BEST
BOY OR GIRL RIDER".

notice of your pony, at the end, as in front, but also keep a good space between the next person and yousself so that the Judge can see your pony's movements better, and if those who want to hurry on in front, always let them pass on the left side, or the judge will not notice you. But you must start teaching your pony all about showing a good time beforehand. Before you enter the ring you must see that your pony's saddlery, and so on is all right and that he is looking his very best! it is a good thing to brush his tail and mane with water. as this makes them smooth and glossy. Then mount, stirrups not too short and your cane held in the right hand, and, do not forget your number card which should be tied round the back, or, arm,. turn his head away from the crowd for a few minutes and walk him up and down, and, if you have not already done so, talk to him soothingly, and explain what he has got to do, and I assure you he will do his very best.! Now, go back when the other competitors are collecting beside the ring.

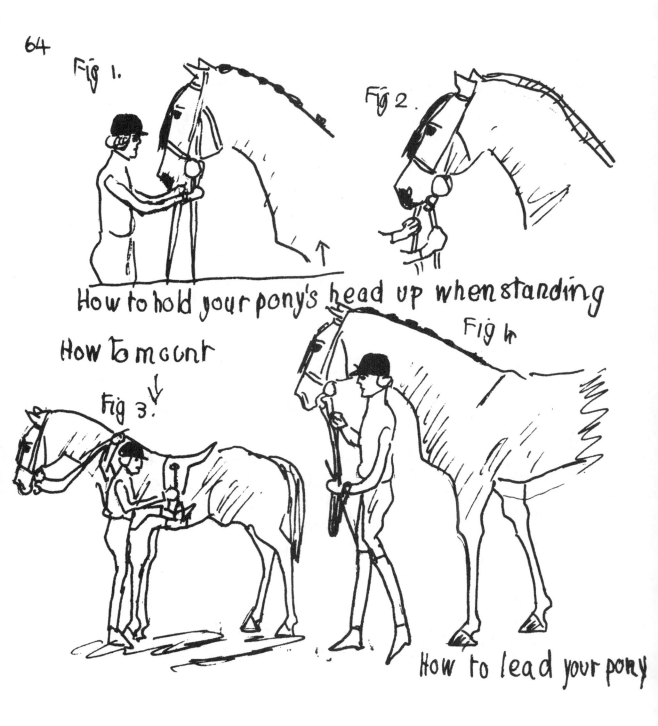

Fig 1.

Fig 2.

How to hold your pony's head up when standing

How to mount

Fig 3.

Fig 4

How to lead your pony

and just wait quitely till you
go in, have your reins not too
short, and your hands well in, and
down, one usualy goes at a walk
along one side of the ring. till
all the competitors have filed in,
so keep your pony going nicely with
his head well up and just sit as
still and quiet as you can, with your
elbows and toes well in, then when
they start to trot ease his mouth
sit up, and just keep going steadily,
as they start to 'canter' keep your
hands well down sit quite still and
keep his legs under him. you will
then probably be called in if you are
lucky and stand beside the line
of other ponies that have been
picked out, always listen hard and
obey at once whatever the judge
tell you. You may then have to
get your saddle off, slip quickly
to the ground, and take place if

gently ton the ground then stand
in front of your pony and hold
the reins as shown in Fig 1. on page
48. either with the reins on, or over
his head. If the juge tells you to come
out and show his paces, slip the
reins over his head like Fig 4 (holding
your stick in the left hand) and
make him trot up and down till
you are told to go back, always
remember when you get to the
end do turn to the right away from
you or your pony will get out of step.
If your pony is given a rosette tie
it either to his head band or the cheek
strap, but if you have not time place
it between your teeth. Never gallop
round the ring when you have had a
ribbon always canter. If you are
showing at Olympia, boys, take your
hats off the second time round, and
if you are given a ribbon, girls, you
cannots do this, but smile sweetly at
the Judge and hope for the best!

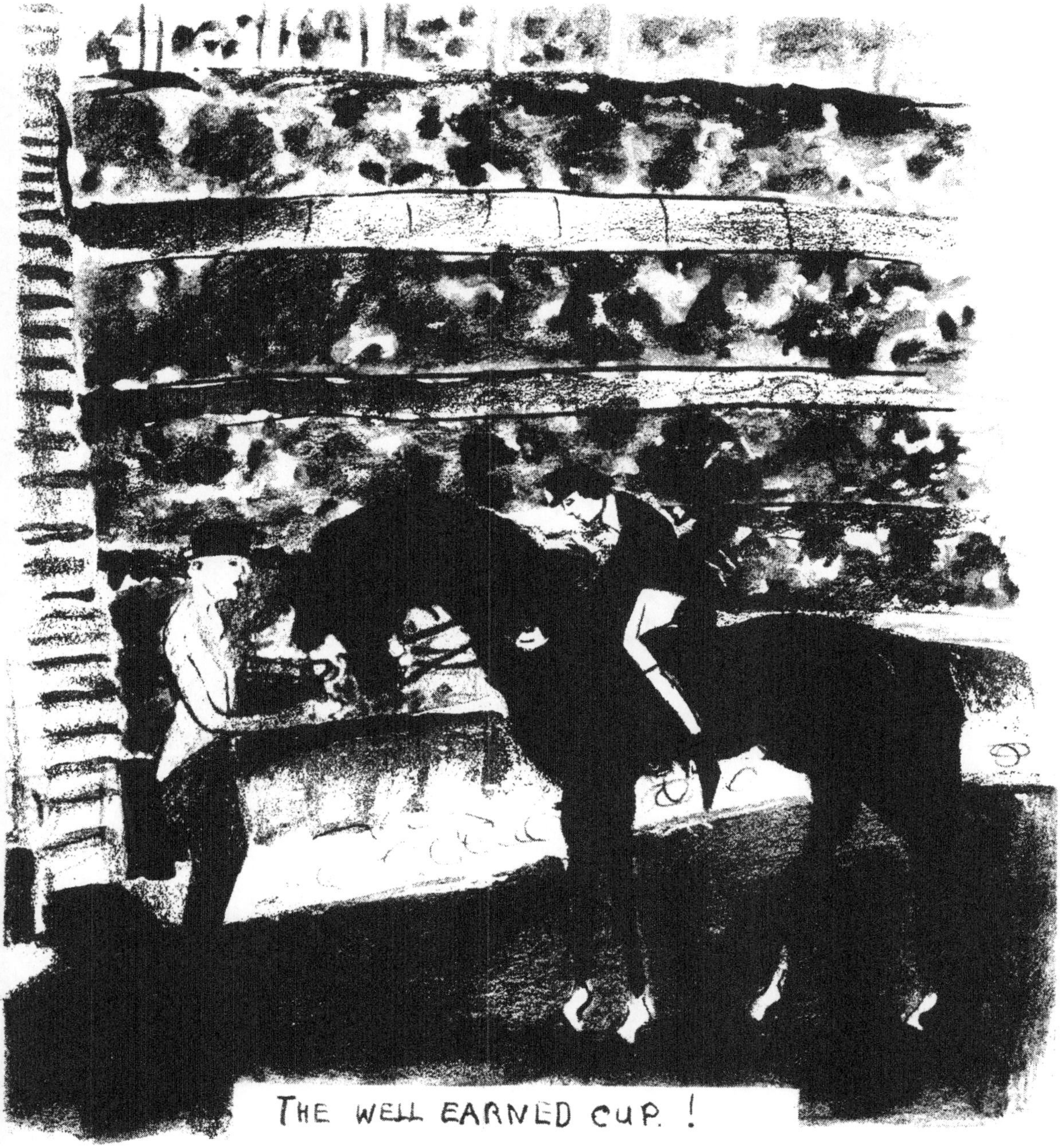

THE WELL EARNED CUP !

CHAPTER IX.

SHOW JUMPING

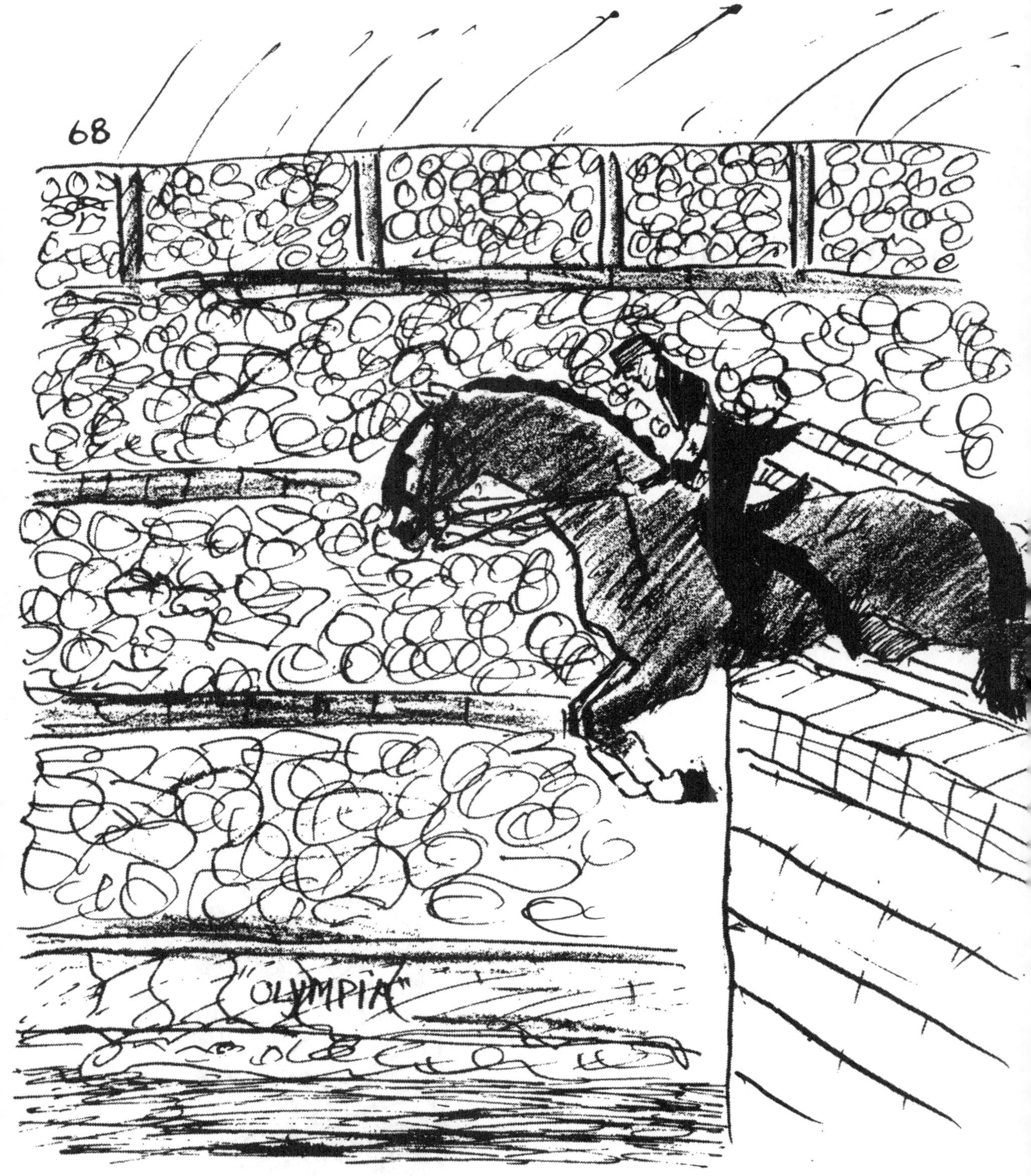
"OLYMPIA"

If you, my reader, have ever seen the army teams jumpy at the Horse show, Olympia, you will thenknow what a realy stiff show jump is like and how to tackle it. Notice how they time their horses exactly, and their bodies just moove together with their horses. To see realy good high jumping is a glorious thing, if you have ever been to Olympia you will remember when the big doors open for each competitor as they enter the arena, easing up as they go for the first jump, the trIpple bar, over with a bound—onward swiftly to the next—— over! then bending graeefuly to the right and round—— a good effort over the gate! —— onward, over, round, sweeping down to the next! —— cleared, —— now for the last, steady! ov——! crash! "Ah! bad luck!" onlookers, and again the huge doors open, to hide the good old brown!.. you must also notice how the riders lean pretty far forward and come down, right on their horse's heads. This is called the "Forward seat"

But if you are not going over
realy high jumps, like at Olympia
there is no need to do it, as well
as being not quite so beeoming
for children! especialy if they do
it not quite right.___ as they
may tip themselves right over their
ponies necks! For usual, children's
jumping classes, the jumps are not
much over 3ft. 6", so if you are going
to practice up for a prize, you
must try putting your pony (without
help) over the following:

"BRUSH". fence. above hight.

"GATE"   "   "

"WALL". wood blocks. "   "

"Bars". triple.   "   " as These
are usualy what the jumps consist
of, and of course, in the ring,
you will find that there are little thin
pieces of wood on top of all the jumps
and, at the least touch, sometimes even
the wind, they fly off!

72 If you go over a brush fence first, Fig 1. page 56
let him go at it at a good pace, collect
him, and make him take off near the
jump, as you will want his lenth over a
wide obstacle. For the "gate" and "wall" Figs. 2.3
You must steady him up a bit more,
as here you want his hieght, and
take off a little farther away, for timber,
you must always have your pony in
hand, and well collected.   For the
(Fig4) "tripple bars" get him going at a good
pace, Also, above all never let him
get excited at any jump or this would
prove fatal! If you are one of those girls
and boys who have got a prize for jumping
a show or even Olympia never boast that
you have won it, on the contrary, put the
pony you rode then first, also, it is quite
true, if you had'nt your pony to help you, you
would never have won, if he did not feel
like "jumping" you could'nt clear the obstacles
and all would be lost, and if you have got
a shinning cup on the mantlepiece in your
room alway say—it is by him that you
possess it.

Fig 1. BRUSH

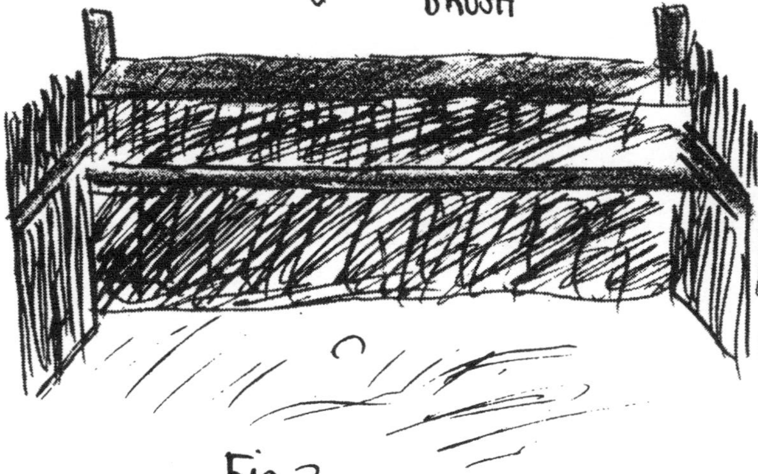

Fig 2.

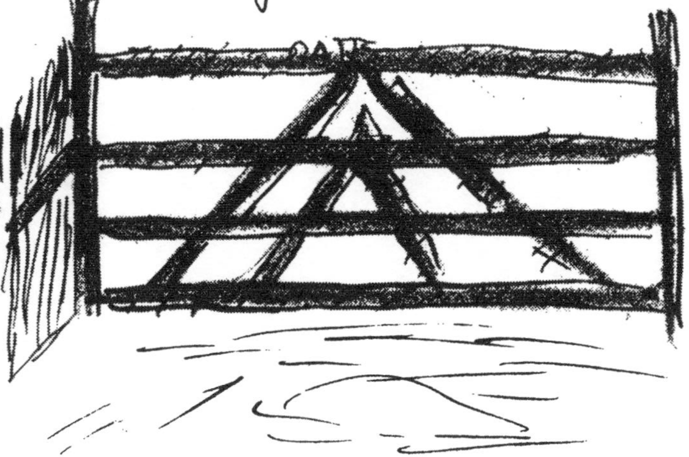

Fig 3

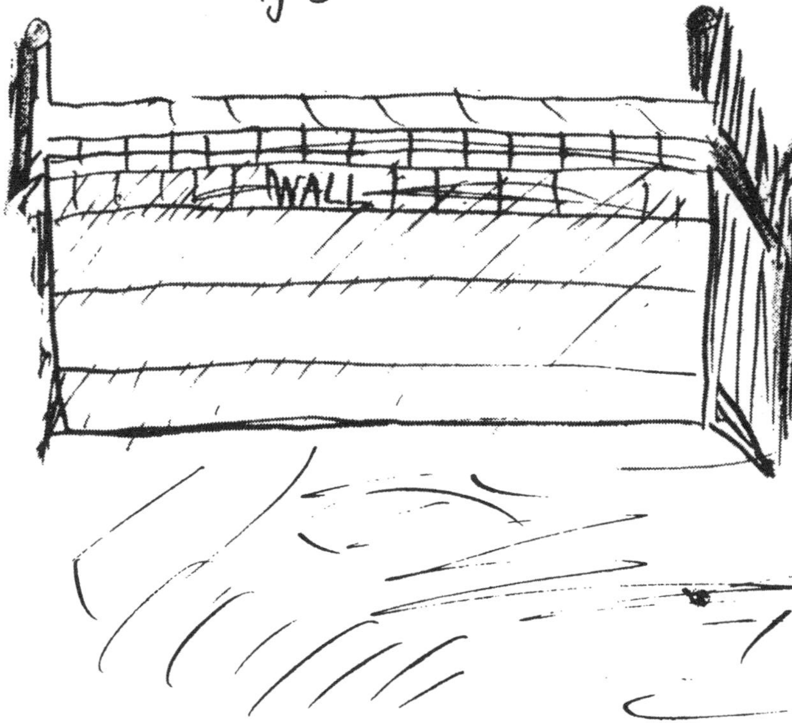
WALL

Fig 4. TRIPPLE BARS

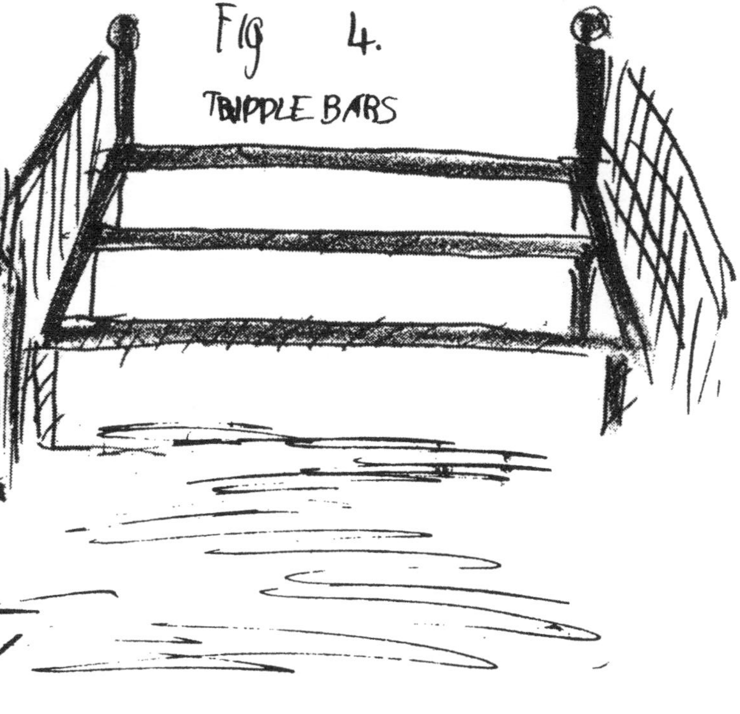

CHAPTER X

HUNTING

Perhaps you are one of those people who live in a very good hunting county,—then think yourself very lucky indeed! But, perhaps, you may live in a very bad one,—— that is hard luck!, though, if you are a good sportsman, you can get just as much fun, and just as good a run as you would if you were hunting with the Beroir or Warickshire etc. Now then A go and fix up a good day with your father! We will start from the begginmg.

Always have a very good break fast, as you will only have your sandwiches for lunch, it is a godd thing to have some ginger biscuits etc. in as well as they do not crumble so much as sandwiches, and, take a few bits of plain chocolate to eat for the hack home.

Now, have you got all the things on the next page?

You must always start early, for the meet, so that you will not be late if you are delayed on the way.

When you get there, go and find your pony, and don't forget your sandwich case! If your hostess asks you in, always go and have some coffee, it is rolte not too. Always say "Good morning"

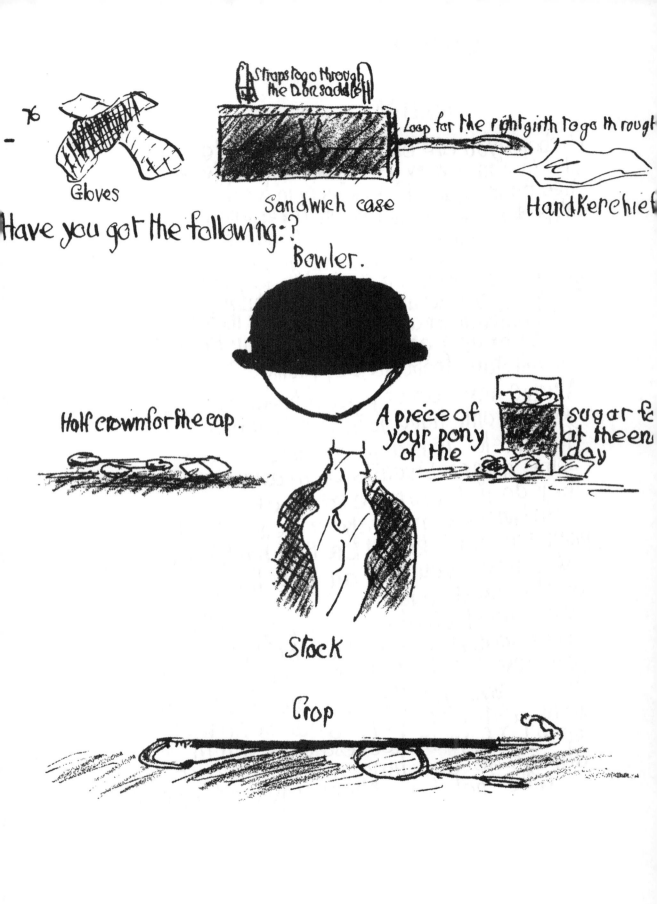

Gloves

Straps to go through the D. or saddle

Loop for the right girth to go through

Sandwich case

Handkerchief

Have you got the following:?

Bowler.

Half crown for the cap.

A piece of your pony of the

sugar & at the end day

Stock

Crop

to the Master, and then the Hunt Servants.
When they move off, dont ride too near
the hounds, and beware of bigger horses,
they do not always like ponies,—so,
"Ware Heels".!
Sit quitely outside cover, while the hounds
draw, then, if you hear a "gone away!"
you can show what stuff you and your
pony are made of!, but, always remember
to spare him as much as possible, you
never know when you may want his speed
again next. If you have started on a good
run that's likely to continue do as the motto
says, and,—— "ride strait for nature's true timber
however strong"! but on the other hand,
if you are one of the "gate brigade" you
cannot do this. Never take a jump.
unessarly   . If you hear "hounds gentlemen
please" turn your pony so that his heels
are away from them. Manners count so
much in the hunting field, so be on your
best behavior! If there is a gate to be opened

be the first to jump off. But, if someone is there before you, go through quickly, with a "thank-you", dont waste his time. If you have a fall, jump up quickly catch your pony, and scramble on again, and if someone has caught him for you thank him and get on at once. Never be a nuisance to others. If your pony gets tired before the end of the day turn home, you do not want to miss another hunt, and he might very likely go lame after a bit and then you might not be able to take him out for weeks, that, would be a great pity wouldn't it? Therefore always think of your pony before yourself, and ride him gently home. If it is a wet day and you can't hunt never show your disapointment, bear up and look forward to another day. Any way, when you get home from hunting have a hot bath, go to bed, sleep tight, and may you dream of ———— "FOX HUNTING"!

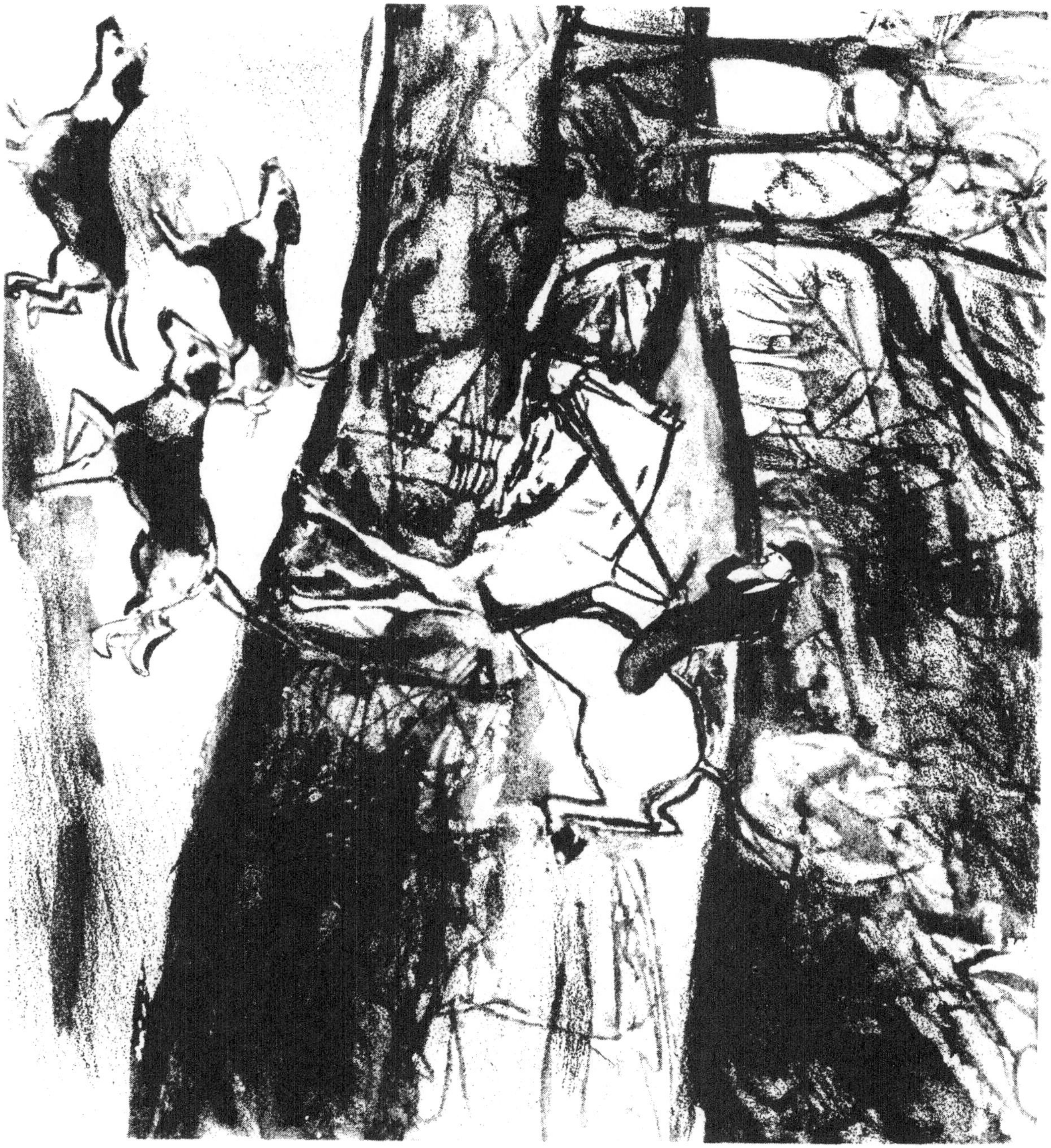

STABLE MANAGEMENT
Chapter XI

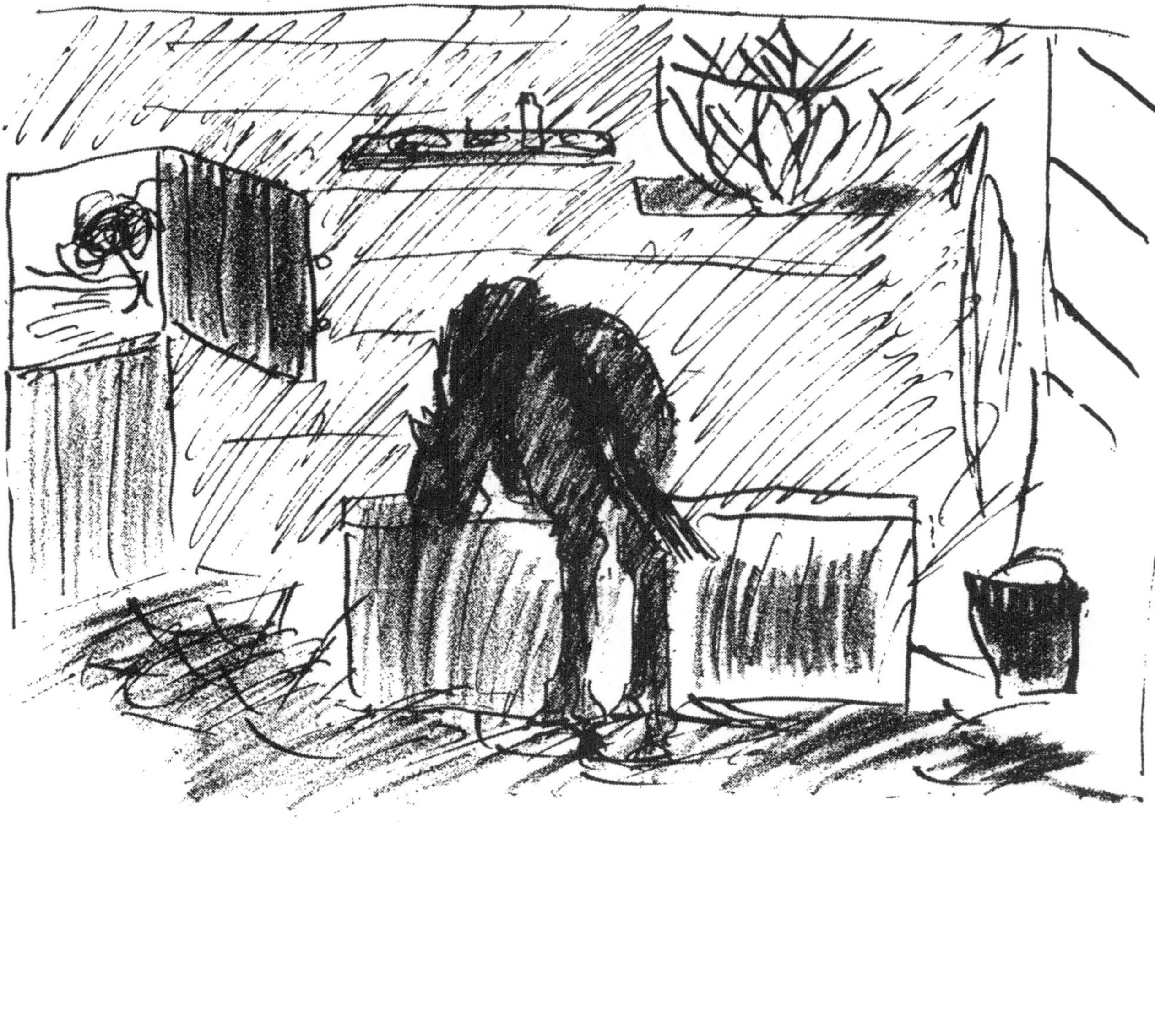

To begin with, your stable must
always be, dry, clean, warm, and
fresh. Some stables smell horrible,
dirty, musty, and badly drained.
On no acount must you let your
pony be in a stable like this. Have
plenty of light clean straw for a
bed and it should be made, and
changed frequently. But, some horses
have a bad habit of eating their
beds, so in this case sawdust etc.
is a good thing. The stable should
always be very airy, there is a
special door, that the top part can
be left open, as on opisite page, and
there should be plenty of water at
hand. It is very useful to have
a few shelves high up to put all
the cleaning things etc. on, but

Legging up a novice.

some stables have a harness room
where one can keep all these things
In the harness room one can keep the
saddles, which should be on a horse.
see page 16. or on pegs round the room
— bridles, stirrups etc, which are
all cleaned there. The walls are
usualy covered, if a big stable, with
the rosettes won by the horses
belonging there. There is also a
stove by which one drys the saddles
etc. after they have got wet. It is
thus rather an attractive place!
especialy when, just as you are
entering, the smell of leather, polish
and other odours come to your
nostrils!

COLOURS AND KINDS

Chapter XII

Greys

A   horse that is quite white is called a _____ { "grey"
  "   "   "   "white with black markings _____ { "dapple"
  "   "   "   " a pinky yellowy white _____ { "cream"

Browns

A horse that is a dark brown, a _____ { "brown"
  "   "   "   "   " bright "   " _____ { "bay"
  "   "   "   is a bright yellowy ginger brown, { "chestnut"
  "   "   "   " " bright brown with white patches — { "skewbald"

"Blacks

A horse that is a pure black is called a, _____ { black
  "   "   "   " black with white patches, _____ { "piebald"

Roans

A horse that is a sort of pinky colour a "roan"
there are three kinds a _____ { "silver" roan
                                   { "blue" roan

The most common kind among horses are —
"Brown" — and the most uncommon are — "roans"
Bay   Pure grey
chestnut   cream
black   skewbald
                                 piebald

A pure "grey" is usualy old as the "dapple" turns quite white in later years.

A chesnut is very hot spirited.

The following are nearly always placed in the show ring ———

"Brown
Bay
Chesnut
Black   and   somehow a "grey" hardly ever gets "first"
Roans
Skewbalds (liver and white)
Piebalds (black and white)

"Creams" are seldom seen in the show ring although some of their kind can be very beautiful ponies

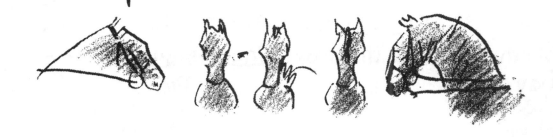

The following kinds are rather a
mix up.

the "Shetland pony comes from the Shetland Isles
 ''   Exmoor   ''   ''   ''   wild Exmoor
 ''   Newforest   ''   ''   ''   the sweet grassy Newforest
 ''   Arab   ''   ''   the deserts of Arabia
There are two kinds of well known hunters
 "English hunter
 Irish   ''   the latter is usualy very good
at tackling walls, and banks, which are the
chief obstacles out there.
A <u>polo</u> pony is about 15 hands
A <u>hunter</u> is about from over 15 to 16 hands
A <u>pony</u> is usualy about from 13 to 15 hands
 or under 13 to 14 hands

"My book is now finished, I have, in all the former pages tried to tell you about the most useful things to learn in horsemanship, it told you very brefly, but I hope you have understood, especialy begginers in ridding, as I have written it also for their pony's sakes too. I think the poem on the opisite page is very like a faithful old hunter who has earned her rest, but even though she had not carried the huntsman to hounds for a long time her heart still yearned towards the sound of the horn! Always be thoughtful for your pony and see that he is always just as happy as you, and, above all, try to make him love you, then he will do anything for you, it is done by kindness and good treatment.

"Love stands through all
And wins the day"!

S Bowes Lyon

The skies are dull, a frosty air,
The dew still lingers on the grass
Till the hounds brush them as they
pass,
With the huntsman on his mare.
At the meets the people say
'Look, here comes Will's gallant
grey
Who's going strong and well this day,
And always first to "get away"!

The hounds against the ridge
were seen
And the scent before them fresh
and keen.
Fences and fields are flashing by,
And o're them all the mare will
fly!
Not one was with them at the death
Huntsman and hounds alone were
left!
Amongst them stood the old grey
mare
In all their joys she had a share.

Those happy days have long since
past
And now the huntsman's horse
has gone,
No more to lead the hounds so fast.
Now all her faithfull work is done.
Now in a field beneath the trees
The hunter still will stand and dream,
The air is full of humming bees
And bubbling onward goes the stream.

Oft she will turn and raise her
head
When far away she hears a sound,
And at some pulsing streak of red
The gallant heart again will bound!
And yearns once more for horn
and hound!

S Bowes-Lyon

NEW YORK: E. P. DUTTON & CO. INC.

ALL RIGHTS RESERVED

MADE AND PRINTED BY THE REPLIKA PROCESS

IN GREAT BRITAIN BY

PERCY LUND, HUMPHRIES & CO. LTD.

12 BEDFORD SQUARE, LONDON, W.C.1

AND AT BRADFORD

FOR

J. M. DENT & SONS LTD.

ALDINE HOUSE, BEDFORD STREET, LONDON, W.C.2

TORONTO   VANCOUVER

MELBOURNE   WELLINGTON

FIRST PUBLISHED

1933

REPRINTED

1933 (*twice*)

CPSIA information can be obtained at www.ICGtesting.com
Printed in the USA
LVOW03*1917290914

406388LV00021B/1208/P